The Chocolate Cookbook

by
Culinary Arts Institute

Dover Publications, Inc.

New York

Published in Canada by General Publishing Company, Ltd., 30 Lesmill Road, Don Mills, Toronto, Ontario.

Published in the United Kingdom by Constable and Company, Ltd., 10 Orange Street, London WC2H 7EG.

This Dover edition, first published in 1988, is a republication of the work originally published by Culinary Arts Institute, Chicago, Illinois, in 1955. The halftones and some of the decorative line art have been omitted and the format has been altered; the text is complete.

Manufactured in the United States of America
Dover Publications, Inc.
31 East 2nd Street
Mineola, N.Y. 11501

Library of Congress Cataloging-in-Publication Data

The Chocolate cookbook / by the Culinary Arts Institute.
     p. cm.
  Reprint. Originally published: Chicago : Culinary Arts Institute, 1955.
  Includes index.
  ISBN 0-486-25770-3 (pbk.)
  1. Cookery (Chocolate)   I. Culinary Arts Institute.
TX767.C5C485   1988
641.6'374—dc19   88-14980
                                                       CIP

Contents

Chocolate Supreme

Ethel Jacobson

When I like chocolate,
I like *chocolate:*
Chocolate cake with chocolate icing
Almost too gooey and rich for slicing;
Chocolate waffles, chocolate mousse;
Chocolate Alaska, chocolate *russe;*
Black-bottom pie, black-topped to match,
With—in the middle—more chocolate, natch.

For when I say chocolate,
I mean *chocolate:*
At breakfast for a wake-up drink,
At midnight on insomnia's brink;
(And what in-between snack's half so dandy
As chocolate-covered chocolate candy?)
Chocolate sundaes; chocolate Mondays;
Maybe chocolate salmagundis.
(Though somehow I've not tried chocolate yet
On asparagus or a lamb *noisette,*
It might be a brand-new taste delight.
I believe I'll try it this very night!)

For when I want chocolate,
I want *chocolate!*
Let doctors scowl, let dentists rave,
Chocolate's the onliest thing I crave;
And happy am I to spy that treat
And take the bitter with the sweet.

Chocolate

Joseph Auslander and Audrey Wurdemann

Can you hear that word without getting your mouth set for something sweet? Chocolate cake, chocolate pie, chocolate pudding, chocolate ice cream, and chocolate sirup on vanilla ice cream! Any boy old enough to go acourting knows that a box of chocolates paves the path to romance; any mother knows that a chocolate-coated pill is far more acceptable to youngsters than plain medicine. There's nothing better on a frosty evening than a cup of hot chocolate topped off with whipped cream, or a frothy cup of cocoa, fragrant and steaming.

IT'S SMART TO BE CAREFUL

THERE'S NO SUBSTITUTE FOR ACCURACY

Read recipe carefully.

Assemble all ingredients and utensils.

Select pans of proper kind and size. Measure inside, from rim to rim.

Use standard measuring cups and spoons. Use measuring cups with subdivisions marked on sides for liquids. Use graduated nested measuring cups for dry or solid ingredients.

Check liquid measurements at eye level.

Sift (before measuring) regular all-purpose flour, or not, in accord with the miller's directions on the package. When using the instant type all-purpose flour, follow package directions and recipes. Level flour in cup with straight-edged knife or spatula. Spoon, without sifting, whole-grain types of flour into measuring cup.

Level dry measurements with straight-edged knife or spatula.

Preheat oven at required temperature.

Beat whole eggs until thick and piled softly when recipe calls for well-beaten eggs.

FOR THESE RECIPES—WHAT TO USE

BAKING POWDER—double-action type.

BREAD CRUMBS—two slices fresh bread equal about 1 cup soft crumbs or cubes. One slice dry or toasted bread equals about ½ cup dry cubes or ¼ cup fine, dry crumbs.

CHOCOLATE—unsweetened chocolate. A general substitution for 1 sq. (1 oz.) chocolate is 3 to 4 tablespoons cocoa plus 1 tablespoon shortening.

CHOCOLATE (no melt)—1-oz. packets or envelopes chocolate-flavored product or ingredient.

CORNSTARCH—thickening agent having double the thickening power of flour.

CREAM—light, table or coffee cream containing 18% to 20% butterfat.

HEAVY or WHIPPING CREAM—containing not less than 30% butterfat.

FLOUR—regular all-purpose flour. When substituting for cake flour, use 1 cup minus 2 tablespoons all-purpose flour for 1 cup cake flour.

GRATED PEEL—citrus fruit peel finely grated through colored part only.

HERBS AND SPICES—ground unless recipe specifies otherwise.

ROTARY BEATER—hand-operated (Dover-type) beater, or use electric mixer.

SHORTENING—a hydrogenated vegetable shortening, all-purpose shortening, butter or margarine. Use oil or lard when specified.

SOUR MILK—sweet milk added to 1 tablespoon vinegar or lemon juice in a measuring cup to fill to 1-cup line; stir. Or use buttermilk.

SUGAR—granulated (beet or cane).

VINEGAR—cider.

HOW TO DO IT

BLANCH NUTS—The flavor of nuts is best maintained when nuts are allowed to remain in water the shortest possible time during blanching. Therefore, blanch only about ½ cup at a time; repeat process as many times as necessary for larger amounts.

Bring to rapid boiling enough water to well cover shelled nuts. Drop in nuts. Turn off heat and allow nuts to remain in the water about 1 min.; drain or remove with fork or slotted spoon. Place between folds of absorbent paper; pat dry. Gently squeeze nuts with fingers or peel to remove skins. Place on dry absorbent paper. To dry thoroughly, frequently shift nuts to dry spots on paper.

TOAST NUTS—place nuts in a shallow baking pan. Heat nuts (plain or brushed lightly with cooking oil, in oven at 350°F until delicately browned. Stir and turn occasionally. Or add nuts to a heavy skillet in which butter or margarine (about 1 tablespoon per cup of nuts) has been melted; or use oil. Brown lightly over moderate heat, constantly moving and turning with spoon.

SALT NUTS—toast nuts; drain on absorbent paper and sprinkle with salt.

BOIL—cook in liquid in which bubbles rise continually and break on the surface. Boiling temperature of water at sea level is 212°F.

BROWN SUGAR—to measure, pack firmly into dry measuring cup so that sugar will hold shape of cup when turned out. To measure granulated brown sugar, see substitution table on package before pouring into measuring cup.

MELT CHOCOLATE—unsweetened, over simmering water; milk, sweet or semi-sweet, over hot (not simmering) water.

CUT MARSHMALLOWS OR DRIED (uncooked) FRUITS—with scissors dipped frequently in water.

FLUTE EDGE—press index finger on edge of pastry, then pinch pastry with thumb and index finger of other hand. Lift fingers and repeat procedure to flute around entire edge.

FOLD—use flexible spatula and slip it down side of bowl to bottom. Turn bowl quarter turn. Lift spatula through mixture along side of bowl with blade parallel to surface. Turn spatula over to fold lifted mixture across material on surface. Cut down and under; turn bowl and repeat process until material seems blended. With every fourth stroke bring spatula up through center.

CHILL GELATIN—set dissolved gelatin mixture in refrigerator or pan of ice and water until slightly thicker than consistency of thick, unbeaten egg white, stirring occasionally. (If placed in pan of ice and water, stir frequently; if placed in refrigerator, stir occasionally.)

PREPARE QUICK COFFEE—for one cup coffee beverage, place one teaspoon concentrated soluble coffee (instant) into cup. Add boiling water and stir until coffee is completely dissolved.

SCALD MILK — heat in top of double boiler over simmering water or in a heavy saucepan over direct heat just until a thin film appears.

SIEVE — force through coarse sieve or food mill.

SWEETEN WHIPPED CREAM — beat thoroughly chilled whipping cream in chilled bowl with chilled rotary beater; beat until cream stands in peaks when beater is slowly lifted upright. With final strokes, beat in ¼ cup sifted confectioners' sugar and 2 teaspoons vanilla extract for each cup of whipping cream.

WATER BATH (HOT) — set a deep pan on oven rack and place the filled baking dish in pan. Surround with very hot water to at least 1-in. depth.

OVEN TEMPERATURES

Very Slow	250°F to 275°F
Slow	300°F to 325°F
Moderate	350°F to 375°F
Hot	400°F to 425°F
Very Hot	450°F to 475°F
Extremely Hot	500°F to 525°F

Use a portable oven thermometer to double-check oven temperature.

WHEN YOU BROIL

Set temperature control of range at Broil. Distance from top of food to source of heat determines intensity of heat upon food.

WHEN YOU COOK CANDY OR SIRUP

A candy thermometer is an accurate guide to correct stage of cooking. Put the thermometer into sirup mixture after sugar is dissolved and boiling starts. A 3-in. depth of sirup is advisable to take an accurate thermometer reading; if necessary, tip pan to obtain this depth. If thermometer is cold, heat it in warm water before plunging it into the hot sirup.

Sirup Stages and Temperatures

Thread (230°F to 234°F) — Spins 2-in. thread when allowed to drop from fork or spoon.

Soft Ball (234°F to 240°F) — Forms a soft ball in very cold water; it flattens when removed from water.

Firm Ball (244°F to 248°F) — Forms a firm ball in very cold water; it does not flatten in the fingers.

Hard Ball (250°F to 266°F) — Forms a ball which is pliable yet hard enough to hold its shape in very cold water.

Soft Crack (270°F to 290°F) — Separates into threads which are hard but not brittle in very cold water.

Hard Crack (300°F to 310°F) — Separates into threads which are hard and brittle in very cold water.

Base Recipes are indicated by solid ▲ pyramid. In variations of Base Recipe, open △ pyramid refers to ▲ *Base Recipe* immediately preceding it.

A CHECK-LIST FOR SUCCESSFUL BAKING

√ **READ AGAIN** "It's Smart to be Careful—There's No Substitute for Accuracy" (page 5).

√ **PLACE OVEN RACK** so top of product will be almost at center of oven. Stagger pans so no pan is directly over another and they do not touch each other or walls of oven. Arrange single pan so that center of product is as near center of oven as possible.

√ **PREPARE PAN**—For cakes with shortening and cake rolls, grease bottom of pan only; line with waxed paper cut to fit bottom; grease waxed paper. If cake (plain or frosted) is to be cut and stored in pan, omit waxed paper. For cakes without shortening (sponge type) and chiffon cakes, do not grease or line pan. For cookies, lightly grease cookie sheets. If recipe directs "Set out pan," do not grease or line pan.

√ **HAVE ALL INGREDIENTS** at room temperature unless recipe specifies otherwise.

√ **SIFT** (before measuring) regular all-purpose flour, or not, in accord with the miller's directions on the package. When using the instant type all-purpose flour, follow package directions and recipes. Level flour in cup with straight-edged knife or spatula. Spoon, without sifting, whole-grain types of flour into measuring cup.

√ **CREAM SHORTENING** (alone or with flavorings) by stirring, rubbing or beating with spoon or electric mixer until softened. Add sugar in small amounts, creaming thoroughly after each addition. Thorough creaming helps to insure a fine-grained cake.

√ **BEAT EGG WHITES** as follows: **Frothy**—entire mass forms bubbles; **Rounded peaks**—peaks turn over slightly when beater is slowly lifted upright; **Stiff peaks**—peaks remain standing when beater is slowly lifted upright.

√ **BEAT EGG YOLKS** until thick and lemon colored when recipe calls for well-beaten egg yolks.

√ **WHEN LIQUID AND DRY INGREDIENTS** are added alternately to cake batter, begin and end with dry. Add dry ingredients in fourths, liquid in thirds. After each addition, beat only until smooth. Finally beat only until batter is smooth (do not overbeat). Scrape spoon or beater and bottom and sides of bowl during mixing.

If using an electric mixer, beat mixture at a low speed when adding liquid and dry ingredients.

√ **FILL CAKE** pans one-half to two-thirds full.

√ **TAP BOTTOM OF CAKE PAN** sharply with hand or on table to release air bubbles before placing in oven.

√ **TEST CAKE** when minimum baking time is up. Touch lightly at center; if it springs back, cake is done. Or insert a cake tester or wooden pick in center; if it comes out clean, cake is done.

√ **COOL BUTTER CAKES** 10 min. in pan on cooling rack after removing from oven; cool sponge-type cakes as recipe states.

√ **REMOVE CAKE** from pan after cooling. Run spatula gently around sides of pan. Cover with cooling rack. Invert and remove pan. Turn right side up immediately after peeling off waxed paper. Cool cake completely before frosting.

√ **FILL LAYER CAKES:** Spread frosting or filling over top of bottom layer. Cover with the other layer. Repeat procedure if more layers are used. If necessary, hold layers in position with wooden picks; remove when frosting is set.

√ **FROST FILLED LAYER CAKES:** Frost sides first working rapidly. See that frosting touches plate all around bottom, leaving no gaps. Pile remaining frosting on top of cake and spread lightly.

√ **TEST** for lukewarm liquid (80°F to 85°F) by placing a drop on wrist; it will feel neither hot nor cold.

√ **REMOVE COOKIES** from pans as they come from oven unless otherwise directed. Set on cooling racks.

Cakes

Sour Cream Chocolate Cake

▲ Base Recipe

Prepare (page 7) two 8-in. round layer cake pans.

Combine and melt (page 5)
>   3 oz. (3 sq.) chocolate
>   ½ cup double-strength coffee beverage

Blend thoroughly. Set aside to cool.

Sift together and set aside
>   2 cups sifted cake flour
>   1 teaspoon baking soda
>   ½ teaspoon salt

Beat together
>   1½ cups sugar
>   1 cup thick sour cream
>   2½ teaspoons vanilla extract

Add in thirds, beating thoroughly after each addition
>   2 eggs, well beaten

Add chocolate mixture and mix well. Add dry ingredients in thirds, beating only until batter is smooth after each addition. Finally beat only until batter is smooth (do not overbeat). Turn batter into pans.

Bake at 350°F 35 min., or until cake tests done (page 7). Cool and remove from pans as directed (page 7).

Two 8-in. round layers

—Black Walnut Chocolate Cake

Follow △ Recipe. Stir in ⅔ cup (2⅓ oz.) chopped **black walnuts** with final strokes.

Semi-Sweet Chocolate Cake

Prepare (page 7) two 9-in. round layer cake pans.

Melt (page 5) and set aside to cool
>   9 oz. semi-sweet chocolate

Sift together and set aside
>   2¾ cups sifted cake flour
>   1 tablespoon baking powder
>   ½ teaspoon baking soda
>   ½ teaspoon salt

Cream together until shortening is softened
>   1 cup butter or margarine
>   1 teaspoon vanilla extract

Add gradually, creaming until fluffy after each addition
>   1 cup sugar

Add in thirds, beating thoroughly after each addition
>   4 eggs, well beaten

Stir in cooled chocolate.

Measure
>   ⅔ cup water

Alternately add dry ingredients in fourths, water in thirds, to creamed mixture. After each addition, beat only until smooth. Finally beat only until batter is smooth (do not overbeat). Turn batter into pans.

Bake at 350°F 30 to 35 min., or until cake tests done (page 7). Cool and remove from pans as directed (page 7).

Frost with **Mocha Cocoa Frosting** (page 18).

Two 9-in. round layers

Cherry Chocolate Cake

Prepare (page 7) two 9-in. round layer cake pans.

Melt (page 5) and set aside to cool
>   2 oz. (2 sq.) chocolate

Drain, reserving sirup
>   6-oz. bottle maraschino cherries

Finely chop cherries (about ½ cup, chopped) and set aside.

Coarsely chop and set aside
>   ¾ cup (about 3 oz.) black walnuts or pecans

Sift together and set aside
>   2¼ cups sifted cake flour
>   2 teaspoons baking powder
>   ¾ teaspoon baking soda
>   ¼ teaspoon salt

Cream until shortening is softened
>   ½ cup plus 2 tablespoons butter or margarine

Add gradually, creaming until fluffy after each addition
>   1¼ cups sugar

Add and beat thoroughly
>   1 egg, well beaten

Stir in chocolate.

Combine
>   1¼ cups thick sour cream
>   ¼ cup reserved maraschino cherry sirup

Alternately add dry ingredients in fourths, sour cream mixture in thirds, to creamed mixture. After each addition, beat only until smooth. Finally beat only until batter is smooth (do not overbeat). Blend in the chopped nuts and chopped cherries. Turn batter into cake pans.

Bake at 375°F 30 to 35 min., or until cake tests done (page 7). Cool and remove from pans as directed (page 7).

Two 9-in. round layers

Flower Garden Chocolate Cake

Bring an air of spring to your table with this festive flower cake!!

Prepare (page 7) 13x9x2-in. cake pan.

Combine in top of double boiler and heat over simmering water until milk is scalded (page 6) and chocolate is melted
⅔ cup milk
4 oz. (4 sq.) chocolate
Stir until well blended.

Vigorously stir about 3 tablespoons hot mixture into
1 egg yolk, slightly beaten
Immediately blend into mixture in double boiler. Cook 2 to 3 min., stirring constantly. Add and stir until dissolved
1 cup minus 2 tablespoons sugar
Cook over simmering water, stirring constantly, about 5 min. Remove from simmering water and set aside to cool.

Sift together and set aside
2⅔ cups sifted cake flour
1 tablespoon baking powder
½ teaspoon baking soda
½ teaspoon salt

Cream together until softened
⅔ cup butter
⅓ cup almond paste
2 teaspoons vanilla extract
Few drops red food coloring
Add gradually, creaming until fluffy after each addition
¾ cup firmly packed brown sugar

Add in thirds, beating thoroughly after each addition
4 egg yolks, well beaten
Blend in the chocolate mixture and set aside.

Mix together
⅓ cup water
3 tablespoons milk
Alternately add dry ingredients in fourths, liquid in thirds, to creamed mixture. After each addition, beat only until smooth. Finally beat only until batter is smooth (do not overbeat).

Beat until frothy
3 egg whites
Add gradually, beating well after each addition
⅓ cup sugar
Beat until stiff peaks are formed. Spread beaten egg whites over blended batter and fold (page 5) together. Turn batter into pan.

Bake at 375°F 35 to 40 min., or until cake tests done (page 7). Cool and remove from pan as directed (page 7).

When cake is cooled, prepare
Seven-Minute Frosting (page 19)
Frost sides and top of cake. Spread evenly.

Mark cake into serving-size pieces, then sprinkle with colored sugar. Decorate with fresh garden flowers. Wrap stem of each flower with aluminum foil and place one blossom on each serving. Colored wooden picks or cocktail picks inserted to form "X's" on the top of outer edge of cake form a colorful border for Flower Garden Cake.

18 to 24 servings

Cocoa Angel Food Cake

Set out 10-in. tubed pan.

Measure into a large bowl
1½ cups (about 12) egg whites
Allow to stand at room temperature about 1 hr. before beating. This will insure greater volume.

Meanwhile, sift together 4 times and set aside
1 cup minus 2 tablespoons sifted cake flour
½ cup sugar
⅓ cup cocoa

Measure and set aside
1 cup sugar

Add to egg whites
½ teaspoon salt
Beat with wire whisk, hand rotary beater or electric mixer until frothy. Beat in
1¼ teaspoons cream of tartar
Continue beating until rounded peaks are formed. Add the 1 cup sugar by sprinkling about 3 tablespoons at a time over egg whites and folding only until blended after each addition.

Blend in
1½ teaspoons vanilla extract
Gradually sift flour mixture, about 3 tablespoons at a time, over beaten egg whites. Gently fold (page 7) in dry ingredients after each addition. Slide batter into the pan, turning pan as batter is poured. Cut through batter with knife or spatula to break large air bubbles.

Bake at 350°F about 45 min.

Cake is done if top springs back when lightly touched at center. Immediately invert pan on tubed end on cooling rack until cake is cold. (If cake is higher than pan, invert between two cooling racks so top of cake does not touch any surface.) When cake is cool, with paring knife cut around tube to loosen cake. Loosen sides with spatula and gently remove cake from pan.

One 10-in. tubed cake

Chocolate Mint Roll

Illustrated on front cover

Prepare (page 7) 15½x10½x1-in. jelly roll pan.

Sift together and set aside
> ¾ cup sifted cake flour
> .5 tablespoons cocoa
> ¼ teaspoon salt

Beat until very thick and lemon colored
> 4 egg yolks
> ½ cup sugar
> ¼ cup water
> 1½ teaspoons vanilla extract

Fold (page 5) in dry ingredients. Set aside.

Beat until frothy
> 4 egg whites

Add and beat slightly
> ½ teaspoon cream of tartar

Add gradually, beating well after each addition
> ½ cup sugar

Beat until very stiff peaks are formed. Spread the egg yolk-sugar mixture over the egg whites and gently fold together (page 5) until thoroughly blended. Turn the batter into pan and spread evenly to edges.

Bake at 325°F 30 min., or until cake tests done (page 7). Loosen edges with a sharp knife. Turn immediately onto a towel sprinkled with
> Confectioners' sugar, sifted

Remove waxed paper and cut off any crisp edges of cake.

To roll, begin rolling nearest edge of cake. Using towel as a guide, tightly grasp nearest edge of towel and quickly pull it over beyond opposite edge. Cake will roll itself as you pull. Wrap roll in towel and set on cooling rack to cool (about ½ hr.)

When ready to fill, carefully unroll cooled cake and spread with
> Seven-Minute Peppermint Frosting (one-half recipe, page 19)

Re-roll and sift over top of roll
> 2 to 4 tablespoons confectioners' sugar

One Chocolate Mint Roll

Wee Charm Cakes

▲ *Base Recipe*

Line with paper baking cups or grease bottoms of 36 small muffin pan wells.

Melt (page 5) and set aside to cool
> 2 oz. (2 sq.) chocolate

Sift together and set aside
> 1½ cups sifted cake flour
> 2 teaspoons baking powder
> ¼ teaspoon salt

Cream until shortening is softened
> ½ cup shortening
> 1½ teaspoons vanilla extract

Add gradually, creaming until fluffy after each addition
> 1 cup sugar

Add in thirds, beating thoroughly after each addition
> 2 eggs, well beaten

Blend in melted chocolate.

Measure
> ½ cup milk

Alternately add dry ingredients in fourths, milk in thirds, to creamed mixture. After each addition, beat only until smooth. Finally beat only until batter is smooth. Fill muffin wells two-thirds full.

Bake at 350°F 15 to 20 min., or until cakes test done (page 7). Cool and remove from pans as directed (page 7).

36 small cupcakes

—Cocoa Cakes

Follow △ Recipe, omitting chocolate. Sift in 6 tablespoons **cocoa** with dry ingredients.

—Coconut Balls

Follow △ Recipe or Cocoa Cake recipe. Frost sides and tops with **white or chocolate frosting** and, while moist, roll in moist, shredded **coconut**.

Chocolate Fruit Cake

An exciting, new, chocolate version of the always popular fruit cake.

Two 1½-qt. molds will be needed.

Mix together in a bowl
> ½ lb. (about 1¼ cups) diced, assorted, candied fruits
> ½ lb. candied red cherries, cut in quarters (page 5), (about 1¼ cups, quartered)
> 5 oz. (about 1 cup) golden raisins

Pour over the fruit a mixture of
> ⅓ cup water
> ⅓ cup rum

Cover tightly and allow to stand 8 hrs. or overnight.

Thoroughly grease molds and set aside.

Coarsely chop and set aside
> 2¼ cups (about ¾ lb.) toasted, salted almonds

Melt (page 5) and set aside to cool
> 4 oz. (4 sq.) chocolate

Sift together and set aside
> 2 cups sifted all-purpose flour
> 1 teaspoon baking powder

Beat until thick and lemon colored and set aside
> 6 egg yolks

Cream until softened
> ¾ cup butter

Add gradually, creaming until fluffy after each addition
> 1 cup sugar

Add the beaten egg yolks in thirds, beating thoroughly after each addition.

Stir melted chocolate into creamed mixture. Alternately add dry ingredients in fourths, fruit mixture in thirds, to creamed mixture. After each addition, beat only until batter is blended. Finally beat only until batter is well blended (do not overbeat). Then blend in the chopped nuts.

Beat until frothy
6 egg whites
Add gradually
½ cup sugar
Continue beating until very stiff peaks are formed. Spread beaten egg whites over batter and gently fold (page 5) together. Turn into prepared molds.

Bake at 275°F 1 hr. 45 min. to 2 hrs., or until cake tests done (page 7). Cool completely on cooling rack before removing from pans. Wrap tightly in waxed paper or aluminum foil and store in cool place to age for several weeks before serving. Once or twice a week, using a pastry brush, paint cakes with **rum** and store again.

Two 2½-lb. fruit cakes

Grandmother's Sweet Chocolate Cake

Prepare (page 7) two 8-in. round layer cake pans.

Combine and melt (page 5)
3 oz. sweet chocolate
½ cup boiling water
Blend thoroughly. Set aside to cool.

Sift together and set aside
2 cups sifted cake flour
1 teaspoon baking soda
½ teaspoon salt
Cream together until shortening is softened
½ cup shortening
1 teaspoon vanilla extract
Add gradually, creaming until fluffy after each addition
1 cup sugar
½ cup firmly packed brown sugar
Add in thirds, beating thoroughly after each addition
2 eggs, well beaten

Stir chocolate and blend in; mix well.

Measure
⅔ cup buttermilk
Alternately add dry ingredients in fourths, buttermilk in thirds, to creamed mixture. After each addition, beat only until smooth. Finally beat only until batter is smooth (do not overbeat). Turn batter into pans.

Bake at 375°F 25 to 30 min., or until cake tests done (page 7). Cool and remove from pans as directed (page 7).

Two 8-in. round layers

Chocolate Potato Cake

Prepare (page 7) two 9-in. round layer cake pans.

Wash, pare and cook, covered, in boiling, salted water to cover
2 medium-size (about ⅔ lb.) potatoes
Cook 20 to 30 min., or until tender.

Meanwhile, melt (page 5) and set aside to cool
1 oz. (1 sq.) chocolate

Sift together and set aside
2 cups sifted cake flour
2 teaspoons baking powder
½ teaspoon salt

Drain potatoes and shake pan over low heat to dry thoroughly. Force hot, cooked potatoes through ricer or sieve. Packing lightly, measure
1 cup sieved potatoes
Set aside to cool.

Cream together
1 cup hydrogenated vegetable shortening or all-purpose shortening
2 teaspoons grated lemon peel (page 5)
Add gradually, creaming until fluffy after each addition
2 cups sugar
Add in thirds, beating thoroughly after each addition
4 eggs, well beaten
Stir in the cooled chocolate.

Blend potatoes with
½ cup milk
Alternately add dry ingredients in fourths and potato mixture in thirds to creamed mixture. After each addition, beat only until smooth. Finally beat only until batter is smooth (do not overbeat). Turn batter into pans.

Bake at 350°F 40 to 45 min., or until cake tests done (page 7). Cool and remove from pans as directed (page 7).

Two 9-in. round layers

Note: Grated raw potatoes may be substituted for the cooked ones; grate them just after adding the eggs to the creamed mixture.

Favorite Chocolate Cake

Prepare (page 7) two 9-in. round layer cake pans.

Melt (page 5) and set aside to cool
   3 oz. (3 sq.) chocolate

Sift together and set aside
   2½ cups sifted cake flour
   1 teaspoon baking soda
   ¾ teaspoon salt

Cream together
   ¾ cup lard
   2 teaspoons vanilla extract
Add gradually, creaming until fluffy after each addition
   2 cups sugar
Beat until thick and lemon colored
   5 egg yolks
Add egg yolks to creamed mixture in thirds, beating thoroughly after each addition. Blend in melted chocolate.

Measure
   1 cup sour milk (page 5)
Alternately add dry ingredients in fourths, sour milk in thirds, to creamed mixture. After each addition, beat only until smooth. Finally beat only until batter is smooth (do not overbeat).

Beat until rounded peaks are formed
   5 egg whites
Fold (page 5) egg whites into batter. Turn batter into pans.

Bake at 375°F 30 to 35 min. or until cake tests done (page 7). Cool and remove from pans as directed (page 7).
   Two 9-in. round layers

Featherlight Chocolate Cake

Prepare (page 7) two 9-in. round layer cake pans.

Combine and stir until chocolate is melted
   1½ oz. (1½ sq.) chocolate
   ½ cup boiling water
Set aside to cool.

Sift together and set aside
   2¼ cups sifted cake flour
   1 teaspoon baking powder
   1 teaspoon baking soda
   ¼ teaspoon salt

Cream together until shortening is softened
   ½ cup butter or margarine
   1 teaspoon vanilla extract
Add gradually, creaming thoroughly after each addition
   2 cups firmly packed light brown sugar
Add in thirds, beating thoroughly after each addition
   2 eggs, well beaten
Stir in cooled chocolate mixture.

Measure
   ½ cup sour milk (page 5)

Alternately add dry ingredients in fourths, sour milk in thirds, to creamed mixture. After each addition, beat only until smooth. Finally beat only until batter is smooth (do not overbeat); blend in with last strokes
   1 teaspoon red food coloring
Turn batter into pans.

Bake at 350°F 30 to 35 min., or until cake tests done (page 7). Cool and remove from pans as directed (page 7).
   Two 9-in. round layers

Chocolate Applesauce Cake

Set out 10-in. tubed pan having removable bottom.

Coarsely chop and set aside
   ¾ cup (about 3 oz.) nuts

Sift together and set aside
   3 cups sifted cake flour
   ¾ cup cocoa
   1 tablespoon baking powder
   ½ teaspoon baking soda
   ¾ teaspoon salt
   1½ teaspoons cinnamon
   ¾ teaspoon nutmeg
   ½ teaspoon cloves

Cream together until softened
   ½ cup hydrogenated vegetable shortening or all-purpose shortening
   ½ cup butter
Add gradually, creaming until fluffy after each addition
   1½ cups sugar
Add in thirds, beating thoroughly after each addition
   2 eggs, well beaten

Combine and blend thoroughly
   1 cup thick, sweetened applesauce
   ¾ cup sour milk
Alternately add dry ingredients in fourths, applesauce-sour milk mixture in thirds, to creamed mixture. After each addition, beat only until smooth. Finally beat only until batter is smooth (do not overbeat). Stir in the chopped nuts. Turn batter into pan.

Bake at 350°F about 1 hr., or until cake tests done (page 7).

Remove cake from oven and place onto cooling rack. Allow cake to cool in pan 15 min. Remove tubed section of pan and the cake from the sides of the pan and place onto cooling rack. When cake is cooled, with paring knife cut around tube to loosen cake. Loosen cake from bottom. Gently remove cake.
   One 10-in. tubed cake

Yeast Chocolate Cake

Mixed today and baked tomorrow, this chocolate yeast cake will win everyone's highest approval.

Have available for tomorrow's baking two 8-in. round layer cake pans.

Melt (page 5) and set aside to cool
>**2 oz. (2 sq.) chocolate**

Sift together and set aside
>**2 cups sifted cake flour**
>**1 teaspoon salt**

Cream until shortening is softened
>**½ cup shortening**

Add gradually, creaming until fluffy after each addition
>**1⅓ cups sugar**

Add in thirds, beating thoroughly after each addition
>**2 eggs, well beaten**

Set aside.

Soften
>**1 pkg. active dry yeast**

in
>**¼ cup warm water (110°F to 115°F. If using compressed yeast, soften 1 cake in ¼ cup lukewarm water, 80°F to 85°F.)**

Stir softened yeast and add, along with the cooled chocolate, to the creamed mixture, beating until thoroughly blended.

Measure
>**⅔ cup milk**

Alternately add dry ingredients in fourths, milk in thirds, to creamed mixture. After each addition, beat only until blended. Finally beat only until batter is smooth (do not overbeat). Cover bowl and place batter into refrigerator for at least 6 hours or overnight.

Remove batter from refrigerator and set aside.

Prepare (page 7) the two 8-in. round layer cake pans and set aside.

Mix together until baking soda is dissolved
>**¾ teaspoon baking soda**
>**2 tablespoons warm water**

Immediately blend soda mixture into the batter with
>**·1½ teaspoons vanilla extract**

Turn batter into pans, spreading to edges. Bake at 350°F 25 to 35 min., or until cake tests done (page 7). Cool and remove from pans as directed (page 7).
>*Two 8-in. round layers*

Party Cocoa Cake

▲ *Base Recipe*

Prepare (page 7) two 9-in. round or two 8-in. square layer cake pans.

Mix in a saucepan
>**¾ cup firmly packed brown sugar**
>**¾ cup cocoa**
>**½ cup hot water**

Bring to boiling and then cook slowly for 3 min., or until mixture is slightly thickened; stir constantly. Set aside to cool.

Sift together and set aside
>**2 cups sifted cake flour**
>**1½ teaspoons baking powder**
>**½ teaspoon baking soda**
>**½ teaspoon salt**

Cream together until shortening is softened
>**⅔ cup shortening**
>**1½ teaspoons vanilla extract**

Add gradually, creaming until fluffy after each addition
>**1 cup sugar**

Add in thirds, beating thoroughly after each addition
>**3 eggs, well beaten**

Stir in cooled cocoa mixture.

Measure
>**¾ cup milk**

Alternately add dry ingredients in fourths, milk in thirds, to creamed mixture. After each addition, beat only until smooth. Finally beat only until batter is smooth (do not overbeat). Turn batter into pans.

Bake at 375°F 25 to 30 min., or until cake tests done (page 7). Cool and remove from pans as directed (page 7).

When cake is cooled, prepare
>**Bittersweet Velvet Frosting (page 19)**

Using one-half of frosting, spread over top of one cake layer.

Cut (page 5) into halves
>**32 (about ½ lb.) marshmallows**

Press marshmallows into frosting on cake. Top with second cake layer.

Cut into eighths and blend into remaining frosting
>**8 marshmallows**

Spread frosting over top of second cake layer. Garnish cake corners with
>**2 marshmallows, cut in halves**
>>*Two 9-in. round or*
>>*8-in. square layers*

—Party Mocha Cake

Follow △ Recipe. Substitute ½ cup **double-strength hot coffee beverage** for hot water.

Three-Layer Chocolate Cake

Prepare (page 7) three 9-in. round layer cake pans.

Combine in top of double boiler
    6 oz. (6 sq.) chocolate
    1½ cups boiling water
Cook over simmering water, stirring constantly, until chocolate is melted and mixture thickens. Set aside to cool.

Sift together and set aside
    4 cups sifted cake flour
    1½ teaspoons baking soda
    1 teaspoon baking powder
    1 teaspoon salt

Cream together
    1 cup hydrogenated vegetable shortening or all-purpose shortening
    2½ teaspoons vanilla extract
Add gradually, creaming until fluffy after each addition
    3 cups sugar
Add in thirds, beating thoroughly after each addition
    4 eggs, well beaten

Measure
    ⅔ cup sour milk (page 5)
Alternately add dry ingredients in fourths, sour milk in thirds, to creamed mixture. After each addition, beat only until smooth. Stir in chocolate mixture. Finally beat only until batter is smooth (do not overbeat). Turn batter into pans.

Bake at 350°F 30 to 35 min., or until cake tests done (page 7). Cool and remove from pans as directed (page 7).

When cake is cool prepare
    Seven-Minute Chocolate Frosting (one and one-half times recipe, preparing only one full or one-half recipe at a time, page 19)
Fill and frost (page 7).

Three 9-in. round layers

Meltaway Whipped Cream Cake

Prepare (page 7) two 9-in. round layer cake pans.

Set a bowl and rotary beater in refrigerator.

Sift together and set aside
    2 cups sifted cake flour
    1½ cups sugar
    8 tablespoons cocoa
    1 tablespoon baking powder
    ½ teaspoon salt

Using the chilled bowl and beater, beat until cream stands in peaks when beater is slowly lifted upright
    1 cup chilled whipping cream

Beat until rounded peaks are formed
    3 egg whites
Gently but thoroughly fold (page 5) together whipped cream and beaten egg whites. Sift over this mixture the dry ingredients in fourths, alternately folding in with a mixture of
    ½ cup milk
    2 teaspoons vanilla extract
Turn into pans.

Bake at 350°F 25 to 30 min., or until cake tests done (page 7). Cool and remove from pans as directed (page 7).

Two 9-in. round layers

Cocoa-Mallow Cake

Prepare (page 7) two 9-in. round layer cake pans.

Combine in top of double boiler
    20 (⅓ lb.) marshmallows, cut in quarters (page 5)
    ⅔ cup cocoa
    ½ cup hot water
Cook over simmering water until marshmallows are melted, stirring constantly. Set aside to cool.

Sift together and set aside
    2 cups sifted cake flour
    1 teaspoon baking powder
    1 teaspoon salt
    ½ teaspoon baking soda

Cream together until shortening is softened
    ⅔ cup shortening
    2 teaspoons vanilla extract
Add gradually, creaming until fluffy after each addition
    1 cup sugar
Add in thirds, beating thoroughly after each addition
    3 eggs, well beaten
Stir in cooled cocoa mixture.

Measure
    ¾ cup thick sour cream
Alternately add dry ingredients in fourths, sour cream in thirds, to creamed mixture. After each addition, beat only until smooth. Finally beat only until batter is smooth (do not overbeat). Turn batter into pans.

Bake at 350°F 30 to 35 min., or until cake tests done (page 7). Cool and remove from pans as directed (page 7).

Two 9-in. round layers

Quick Honey Fudge Cake

Prepare (page 7) 13x9x2-in. cake pan.

Melt (page 5) and set aside to cool
   3 oz. (3 sq.) chocolate

Coarsely chop and set aside
   ¾ cup (about 3 oz.) nuts

Sift together into large bowl
   2 cups sifted cake flour
   1 teaspoon baking soda
   ½ teaspoon salt
Add to sifted dry ingredients
   ¾ cup firmly packed brown sugar
   ½ cup hydrogenated vegetable shortening or all-purpose shortening

Combine and beat with rotary beater to blend
   1 cup milk
   ¾ cup honey
   2 teaspoons vanilla extract
Add one-half of the milk mixture to flour mixture. Beat vigorously about 300 strokes, or beat with electric mixer on medium speed for 2 min. Scrape sides of bowl occasionally. Add the cooled chocolate, remaining milk mixture and
   2 eggs, unbeaten
Beat as above with about 300 strokes or for 2 min. Stir in the chopped nuts. Pour batter into prepared pan.

Bake at 375°F about 30 min., or until cake tests done (page 7). Cool and remove from pan as directed (page 7).

13 x 9-in. oblong cake

Chiffon Cocoa Cake

   ▲ *Base Recipe*

Set out a 10-in. tubed pan.

Put into a small bowl
   ½ cup cocoa
Add gradually, blending until smooth and set aside to cool
   ¾ cup boiling water

Sift together into a bowl
   1¾ cups sifted cake flour
   1 cup sugar
   1 tablespoon baking powder
   ¾ teaspoon salt
Make a well in center and add in order
   ½ cup cooking (salad) oil
   7 egg yolks, unbeaten
   2 teaspoons vanilla extract
   Cooled cocoa mixture

Beat with rotary beater until smooth. Set aside.

Beat until frothy
   1 cup (7 to 8) egg whites
Add and continue to beat egg whites slightly
   ½ teaspoon cream of tartar
Add gradually, beating well after each addition
   ¾ cup sugar
Beat until very stiff peaks are formed. Slowly pour egg yolk mixture over entire surface of egg whites. Fold (page 5) gently until completely blended. Turn the batter into ungreased pan.

Bake at 325°F 55 min., then at 350°F 10 to 15 min., or until cake tests done (page 7). Invert on cooling rack. Let hang until cold.

For cooling cake and removing from pan see recipe for Feature Cocoa Sponge Cake (page 16).
One 10-in. tubed cake

—-Nut Chiffon Cake

Follow △ Recipe. When egg mixtures are blended, sprinkle 1 cup (about 4 oz.) finely chopped **nuts** over entire surface. Gently fold in with a few strokes.

Marble Cake

Prepare (page 7) 8x8x2-in. cake pan.

Melt (page 5) and set aside to cool
   1½ oz. (1½ sq.) chocolate

Sift together and set aside
   2 cups sifted cake flour
   2 teaspoons baking powder
   ½ teaspoon salt

Cream until shortening is softened
   ½ cup butter or margarine
   2 teaspoons vanilla extract
Add gradually, creaming until fluffy
   1 cup sugar

Measure
   ¾ cup milk
Alternately add dry ingredients in fourths, milk in thirds, to creamed mixture. After each addition, beat only until smooth. Finally beat only until batter is smooth (do not overbeat).

Beat until rounded peaks are formed
   3 egg whites
Gently fold (page 5) into batter. Turn one-half of batter into cake pan. Stir into remaining batter a mixture of cooled chocolate and
   2 tablespoons hot water
   1 tablespoon sugar
   ½ teaspoon baking soda

Spoon chocolate batter on top of batter in pan. Gently lift white batter through chocolate batter until marbled effect is produced.

Bake at 350°F 40 to 45 min., or until cake tests done (page 7). Cool and remove from pan as directed (page 7).

One 8-in. square cake

Feature Cocoa Sponge Cake

Set out 10-in. tubed pan.

Blend together and set aside
**¾ cup sifted cake flour
⅓ cup cocoa**

Combine and beat until thick and lemon-colored (3 to 4 min. with an electric mixer on medium-high speed)
**6 egg yolks
¾ cup sugar
¼ cup water
1½ teaspoons vanilla extract**
Set aside.

Beat until frothy
6 egg whites
Beat in
**½ teaspoon cream of tartar
¼ teaspoon salt**
Add gradually, beating well after each addition
½ cup sugar
Beat until very stiff peaks are formed. Spread the egg yolk mixture over entire surface of beaten egg whites and gently fold together until mixture is completely blended (page 5). Sift about one-fourth of the flour at a time over surface. Fold together gently after each addition. Turn batter into pan.

Bake at 350°F about 45 min., or until cake tests done (page 7). Immediately invert pan on tubed end on cooling rack until cake is cold. (If cake is higher than pan, invert between two cooling racks so top of cake does not touch any surface.) When cake is cool, with paring knife cut around tube to loosen cake. Loosen sides with spatula and gently remove cake from pan. *One 10-in. tubed cake*

Devil's Food Cake

▲ *Base Recipe*

Prepare (page 7) two 8-in. round layer cake pans.

Melt (page 5) and set aside to cool
3 oz. (3 sq.) chocolate
Sift together and set aside
**2 cups sifted cake flour
1 teaspoon baking soda
½ teaspoon salt**
Cream together until shortening is softened
**½ cup butter or margarine
1½ teaspoons vanilla extract**

Add gradually, creaming well after each addition
1½ cups sugar or firmly packed light brown sugar
Add in thirds, beating thoroughly after each addition
2 eggs, well beaten
Stir in cooled chocolate.

Measure
1 cup milk
Alternately add dry ingredients in fourths, milk in thirds to creamed mixture. After each addition, beat only until smooth. Finally beat only until batter is smooth (do not overbeat); blend in with last strokes
½ teaspoon red food coloring
Turn batter into pans.

Bake at 350°F 30 to 35 min., or until cake tests done (page 7). Cool and remove from pans as directed (page 7).
Two 8-in. round layers

Note: Red food coloring or an excess of baking soda will produce a red color. The excess soda also imparts a distinctive flavor.

—Devil's Food Cupcakes

Follow △ Recipe. Use 24 2½-in. muffin-pan wells lined with paper baking cups, or with bottoms greased. Fill each about two-thirds full. Bake at 350°F about 20 min.

Topsy-Turvy Chocolate Cake

Set out 8-in. square cake pan.

Thaw, drain thoroughly and set aside
2 10-oz. pkgs. frozen sliced peaches (about 2 cups, drained)

Melt (page 5) and set aside to cool
2 oz. (2 sq.) chocolate

Meanwhile, melt in the baking pan
¼ cup butter or margarine
Sprinkle over the butter
½ cup firmly packed brown sugar
Arrange the sliced peaches evenly over the sugar. Set pan aside.

Sift together into a large bowl
**1 cup sifted cake flour
¾ cup sugar
1 teaspoon baking powder
¼ teaspoon salt**
Add to sifted dry ingredients
½ cup butter or margarine, softened
Set aside.

Combine and beat with rotary beater to blend
**1 egg, well beaten
⅓ cup milk
1 teaspoon vanilla extract**
Add the milk mixture to flour mixture. Blend; beat vigorously about 300 strokes, or beat with electric mixer on medium speed for 2 min. Scrape sides of bowl occasionally. Add the chocolate. Beat as above 150 strokes or for 1 min. Turn batter into pan over the peaches.

Bake at 350°F 45 to 50 min., or until cake tests done (page 7). Immediately loosen cake from sides of pan. Invert on serving plate. Let pan rest over cake a few seconds so sirup will drain on cake; lift off pan. Serve warm. Garnish with sweetened **whipped cream** (page 6).

One 8-in. square cake

Brown and Gold Cake

Prepare (page 7) two 8-in. round layer cake pans.

Sift together and set aside
> **2½ cups sifted cake flour**
> **2½ teaspoons baking powder**
> **1 teaspoon salt**

Cream together until butter is softened
> **⅔ cup butter**
> **1¼ teaspoons vanilla extract**
> **¼ teaspoon orange extract**
> **½ teaspoon yellow food coloring (optional)**

Add gradually, creaming thoroughly after each addition
> **1½ cups sugar**

Add in thirds, beating thoroughly after each addition
> **3 eggs, well beaten**

Measure
> **1 cup milk**

Alternately add dry ingredients in fourths, milk in thirds, to creamed mixture. After each addition, beat only until smooth. Finally beat only until batter is smooth (do not overbeat). Turn batter into pans.

Bake at 350°F 30 to 35 min., or until cake tests done (page 7). Cool and remove from pans as directed (page 7).

When cake is cool, prepare
> **Glossy Chocolate Frosting (double recipe, page 18)**

Frost cake (page 7) with frosting.

One 8-in. round layer cake

Milk Chocolate Cake

Prepare (page 7) two 8-in. round layer cake pans.

Combine and stir until chocolate is melted
> **4 or 5 oz. milk chocolate, cut in small pieces**
> **½ cup boiling water**

Set aside to cool.

Sift together and set aside
> **2 cups sifted all-purpose flour**
> **2 teaspoons baking powder**
> **½ teaspoon salt**
> **¼ teaspoon baking soda**

Cream together until shortening is softened
> **½ cup butter or margarine**
> **1 teaspoon vanilla extract**

Add gradually, creaming until fluffy after each addition
> **1 cup firmly packed brown sugar**

Add in thirds, beating thoroughly after each addition
> **2 eggs, well beaten**

Stir chocolate mixture and blend into creamed mixture.

Measure
> **½ cup sour milk or buttermilk**

Alternately add dry ingredients in fourths, liquid in thirds, to creamed mixture. After each addition, beat only until smooth. Finally beat only until batter is smooth (do not overbeat). Turn batter into pans.

Bake at 375°F 25 to 30 min., or until cake tests done (page 7). Cool and remove from pans as directed (page 7).

Two 8-in. round layers

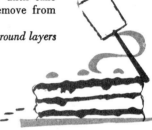

Quick Cocoa Cake

This ring of light-as-a-sunbeam chocolate cake around servings of ice cream is easy to create and always exciting.

Grease bottom of 2-qt. ring mold or prepare (page 7) 8-in. square cake pan.

Sift together into a large bowl
> **1⅓ cups sifted cake flour**
> **1 cup sugar**
> **½ cup cocoa**
> **1 teaspoon baking powder**
> **½ teaspoon baking soda**
> **¼ teaspoon salt**

Add to sifted dry ingredients
> **6 tablespoons hydrogenated vegetable shortening or all-purpose shortening**

Beat with rotary beater to blend and add to flour mixture
> **2 eggs, well beaten**
> **¼ cup milk**
> **1½ teaspoons vanilla extract**

Blend; beat vigorously about 300 strokes, or beat with electric mixer on medium speed for 2 min. Scrape sides and bottom of bowl occasionally.

Blend together and add to batter
> **½ cup milk**
> **2 teaspoons vinegar**

Beat as above about 150 strokes or for 1 min. Pour batter into mold or pan.

Bake at 350°F about 30 min. for ring and 35 min. for square or until cake tests done (page 7). Cool and remove from mold or pan as directed (page 7).

One ring-shape cake or one 8-in. square cake

Frostings and Fillings

Mocha Cocoa Frosting

▲ *Base Recipe*

Sift together
>   3 cups confectioners' sugar
>   ½ cup cocoa

Make a well in center. Add and beat until smooth
>   ½ cup butter or margarine, softened
>   3 tablespoons double-strength coffee beverage

Add and beat well
>   2 egg yolks or 1 whole egg

Spread between layers and on sides and top of cake.

Enough to frost sides and tops of two 9-in. cake layers

—Chocolate Cream Frosting

Follow △ Recipe. Subsitute for coffee, ¼ cup **cream or top milk.**

—Toasted Almond Chip Frosting

Follow △ Recipe. Sprinkle 1 cup (about 5½ oz.) sliced, toasted **almonds** on top and sides of frosted cake.

—Sunshine Chocolate Frosting

Follow △ Recipe. Substitute for coffee, 1 or 2 tablespoons **lemon juice** or **orange juice** with 1 teaspoon **grated peel** (page 5).

Fudge Frosting

▲ *Base Recipe*

Combine in a 3-qt. saucepan
>   4 oz. (4 sq.) chocolate, cut in small pieces
>   3 cups sugar
>   1 cup milk
>   ½ cup butter or margarine
>   2 tablespoons light corn sirup

Heat slowly until boiling briskly, stirring constantly. Cook to 234°F (soft ball stage, page 6; remove from heat while testing). Using a pastry brush dipped in water, wash down the crystals from sides of saucepan from time to time during cooking.

Remove mixture from heat and cool to lukewarm (110°F to 115°F) without stirring or jarring the saucepan. Then add
>   1 tablespoon vanilla extract

Beat until of spreading consistency.

Enough to frost sides and tops of two 8- or 9-in. cake layers

—Mallow Nut Frosting

Follow △ Recipe. Add 1½ cups (about 6 oz.) chopped **nuts** and 8 **marshmallows**, cut in pieces (page 5), after first minute of beating.

Broiler Fudge Frosting

Have ready a hot cake in an 8-in. square pan.

Coarsely chop and set aside
>   ½ cup (about 2 oz.) nuts

Cream until fluffy
>   2 tablespoons butter or margarine, softened
>   ½ cup firmly packed brown sugar
>   2 tablespoons cocoa

Add and continue creaming
>   2 tablespoons cream

Stir in the chopped nuts. Spread lightly over the cake after it has cooled in pan 10 to 15 min.

Set temperature control of range at Broil. Place cake in broiler with top of frosting about 4-in. from source of heat. Broil about 1 min. or until frosting bubbles. Watch closely to avoid scorching.

Enough to frost top of 8-in. square cake

Glossy Chocolate Frosting

▲ *Base Recipe*

Mix thoroughly in a 1-qt. saucepan
>   ½ cup sugar
>   2 tablespoons cornstarch

Stir in
>   ½ cup boiling water
>   1 oz. (1 sq.) chocolate, cut in pieces
>   ¼ teaspoon salt

Cook over medium heat until mixture thickens, stirring frequently. Remove from heat. Stir in
>   2 tablespoons butter or margarine
>   1 teaspoon vanilla extract

Spread on cake while frosting is hot.

Enough to frost tops of two 9-in. cake layers

—Glossy Nut Frosting

Follow △ Recipe. Sprinkle 1 cup (4 oz.) chopped **nuts** on top and sides of frosted cake.

—Glossy Crunch Frosting

Follow △ Recipe. Crush ¼ lb. **peanut or almond brittle.** Stir into frosting before spreading onto cake.

—Glossy Coconut Frosting

Follow △ Recipe. Finely chop 1 cup moist, shredded **coconut**. Stir into frosting before spreading onto cake.

—Glossy Peppermint Frosting

Follow △ Recipe. Crush 6 to 8 small sticks **peppermint candy**. Stir into frosting before spreading onto cake.

Creamy Chocolate Frosting

Melt (page 5) over simmering water and stir until smooth
>   **1 pkg. (6 oz.) semi-sweet chocolate
>   pieces**

Add
>   **⅔ cup sweetened condensed milk**

Cook over low heat 10 min., stirring frequently. Remove from heat. Add and beat until of spreading consistency
>   **2 teaspoons hot water
>   1 teaspoon vanilla extract**

> *Enough to frost sides and tops of
> two 8-in. cake layers or sides and
> top of one 8-in. square cake*

Seven-Minute Chocolate Frosting

▲ *Base Recipe*

Just minutes to the fluffiest, most luscious frosting you ever piled on a cake.

Melt (page 5) and set aside to cool
>   **3 oz. (3 sq.) chocolate**

Combine and mix well in top of double boiler
>   **1½ cups sugar
>   ⅓ cup water
>   1 tablespoon light corn sirup
>   ⅛ teaspoon salt
>   2 egg whites, unbeaten**

Place over boiling water and immediately beat with rotary beater 7 to 10 min., or until mixture holds stiff peaks. Remove from heat. Blend in cooled chocolate and
>   **1 teaspoon vanilla extract**

For Chocolate Swirls—Melt (page 5)
>   **½ oz. (½ sq.) chocolate**

Drop spoonfuls of melted chocolate onto top of frosted cake. Using back of spoon, swirl pools of chocolate.

> *Enough to frost sides and tops
> of two 9-in. cake layers*

—Seven-Minute Peppermint Frosting

Follow △ Recipe. Fold in (page 5) ½ cup (about 6 sticks) finely crushed **peppermint-stick candy** with melted chocolate. If pink frosting is desired, omit chocolate and blend in one or more drops **red food coloring**.

—Seven-Minute Frosting

Follow △ Recipe. Omit chocolate. Increase vanilla extract to 1½ teaspoons.

Bittersweet Velvet Frosting

Melt (page 5) together and stir until smooth
>   **4 oz. (4 sq.) chocolate
>   3 tablespoons butter or margarine**

Remove from heat and add
>   **2¼ cups sifted confectioners' sugar
>   ½ cup top milk or cream
>   1 teaspoon vanilla extract**

Beat until of spreading consistency.

> *Enough to frost sides and tops
> of two 8- or 9-in. cake layers*

Cocoa Whipped Cream

Place rotary beater in refrigerator to chill.

Mix together in a bowl in order
>   **5 tablespoons sugar
>   3 tablespoons cocoa
>   ¼ teaspoon salt
>   1 cup whipping cream
>   2 teaspoons vanilla extract**

Chill in refrigerator 2 hrs. or longer. Whip chilled mixture with chilled rotary beater until cream stands in peaks when beater is slowly lifted upright.

> *Enough to fill 15x10-in. cake roll
> or frost sides and tops of
> two 8-in. cake layers*

Chocolate Bar Frosting

Immediately upon removing cake layers from pans and while cake is warm, place on top of each layer, one-half of
>   **5 semi-sweet or milk chocolate bars
>   (about 2 oz. each)**

As the chocolate melts, quickly spread it around sides and over top of cake layers.

> *Enough to frost sides and tops
> of two 8-in. cake layers*

Mallow Filling

Melt over simmering water
>   **32 marshmallows (about ½ lb.)
>   cut in quarters (page 5)
>   1 oz. (1 sq.) chocolate**

Meanwhile, prepare and set aside
>   **¼ cup (about 1 oz.) raisins, cut in
>   pieces (page 5)
>   ¼ cup (about 1 oz.) chopped nuts
>   ½ teaspoon grated orange or lemon
>   peel (page 5)**

Remove melted marshmallows and chocolate from heat and stir in
>   **1 tablespoon cream**

Blend in the raisins, nuts and grated peel. Stir until filling is of spreading consistency. (Omit chocolate if white filling is desired.)

> *Enough to cover one 8-
> or 9-in. cake layer*

Dusky Cream Cheese Frosting

▲ Base Recipe

Soften
  1 pkg. (3 oz.) cream cheese
Blend in
  ½ teaspoon vanilla extract
Sift together and add gradually
  1 cup confectioners' sugar
  3 tablespoons cocoa
Blend thoroughly. If too stiff to spread, add, 1 teaspoon at a time, until easy to spread
  Milk or cream

Enough to frost one 8-
or 9-in. cake layer

—Chocolate Cream Cheese Frosting

Follow △ Recipe. For cocoa, substitute 1 oz. (1 sq.) **chocolate**, which has been melted

Honey-Chocolate Frosting

Combine in top of double boiler and place over simmering water
  ½ cup sugar
  2 oz. (2 sq.) chocolate, cut in pieces
  ⅓ cup honey
  ¼ cup cream or top milk
  ¼ cup butter or margarine
  ⅛ teaspoon salt
When chocolate is melted, blend well with rotary beater. Vigorously stir about 3 tablespoons of the hot mixture into
  2 egg yolks, slightly beaten
Mix thoroughly and then combine with the mixture in double boiler. Cook over simmering water, stirring constantly. When slightly thickened (about 2 min.), remove from heat; place pan in bowl of ice and water and beat frosting until of spreading consistency.

Enough to frost sides and tops
of two 8-in. cake layers

Sour Cream Chocolate Frosting

Melt (page 5) and cool slightly
  1 pkg. (12 oz.) semi-sweet chocolate pieces
Blend melted chocolate into
  1 cup thick sour cream
Add and blend in
  1 teaspoon vanilla extract
  ¼ teaspoon almond extract
  ⅛ teaspoon salt

Enough to frost sides and tops of
two 8- or 9-in. cake layers

Chocolate Cream Filling

▲ Base Recipe

Heat in double boiler until milk is scalded (page 6) and chocolate melted
  ¾ cup milk
  1 oz. (1 sq.) chocolate

Meanwhile, mix together in a saucepan
  ½ cup sugar
  ¼ cup all-purpose flour
  ¼ teaspoon salt
Stir in and blend well
  ¼ cup cold milk
Gradually add hot milk mixture, stirring constantly. Wash double boiler top to remove scum. Bring chocolate mixture to boiling over direct heat, stirring gently and constantly, and cook about 3 min. Pour into double boiler top and place over simmering water. Cover and cook about 5 to 7 min., stirring occasionally.

Vigorously stir about 3 tablespoons of this hot mixture into
  2 egg yolks, slightly beaten
Immediately blend into mixture in double boiler. Cook over simmering water 3 to 5 min., stirring gently and constantly. Remove from heat and stir in
  1 tablespoon butter or margarine
  1 teaspoon vanilla extract
Cover, cool and chill in refrigerator.

Enough to cover two
8-in. cake layers

—Cocoa Cream Filling

Follow △ Recipe. Omit chocolate. Blend 3 tablespoons **cocoa** with dry ingredients.

—Rum Chocolate Filling

Follow △ Recipe. Blend in 2 teaspoons **rum extract** with the vanilla extract.

Chocolate Marshmallow Frosting

Cut (page 5) into eighths and set aside
  8 marshmallows

Blend well and set aside
  1 cup sifted confectioners' sugar
  2 egg yolks, unbeaten
  ⅛ teaspoon salt

Melt (page 5) together and stir until smooth
  3 oz. (3 sq.) chocolate
  2 tablespoons butter or margarine

Blend together thoroughly and add slowly to melted chocolate mixture
  2½ tablespoons cornstarch
  ⅓ cup cold milk
Immediately stir in egg yolk-sugar mixture. Cook over simmering water about 12 min. Stir frequently. Remove from heat and stir in
  2 teaspoons vanilla extract

When cool, blend in
  1½ cups sifted confectioners' sugar
  Cream, 1 tablespoon at a time, until easy to spread
Remove about one-half of frosting, blend in marshmallows and frost tops of layers. Use plain frosting for sides.

Enough to frost sides and tops of
two 8- or 9-in. cake layers

Cookies

Refrigerator Cookies

▲ Base Recipe

Set out cookie sheet.

Melt (page 5) and set aside to cool
2 oz. (2 sq.) chocolate

Sift together and set aside
3 cups sifted all-purpose flour
2 teaspoons baking powder
½ teaspoon salt

Cream together until blended
1 cup shortening
2 teaspoons vanilla extract
Add gradually, creaming until fluffy after each addition
1 cup sugar
Add in thirds, beating thoroughly after each addition
2 eggs, well beaten
Add flour mixture in fourths and mix thoroughly after each addition. Divide dough into halves. To one-half the dough, stir in melted chocolate and
1 tablespoon milk
Wrap each half of dough in waxed paper and chill in refrigerator until easy to handle. Shape both white and chocolate dough into 2 rolls, each 2 in. in diameter. Again wrap in waxed paper and chill. Cut into ⅛-in. slices.

Bake on ungreased sheet at 400°F 5 to 9 min.
10 doz. cookies

—Cocoa Refrigerator Cookies

Follow △ Recipe. Substitute ½ cup **cocoa** for chocolate; sift cocoa in with the dry ingredients decreasing flour to 2½ cups. Blend in after the flour mixture ½ cup (2 oz.) chopped **nuts** (or ½ cup [2¾ oz.] slivered, toasted, **almonds**, page 5).

—Orange Refrigerator Cookies

Follow △ Recipe. Substitute **orange juice** for milk and add 1 teaspoon grated **orange peel** (page 5).

—Variety Tray

Follow △ Recipe using one-third of each dough for plain cookies. Make up remaining two-thirds in Pinwheels and Stripers.

—Pinwheels

Follow △ Recipe. After chilling dough enough to handle, divide each dough into three por-
tions. Roll one-third of the chocolate and one-third of the white dough into rectangular sheets 8x6x⅛-in. Place chocolate sheet on top of white sheet and roll up tightly into a roll. Repeat process, forming two additional rolls.

—Stripers

Follow △ Recipe. Divide each dough into six portions. Roll two portions of the chocolate dough into 2 squares, ¼ in. thick. Roll two portions of the white dough in the same way. Line a flat pan with waxed paper. Stack layers in pan alternating colors and brushing each layer with slightly beaten **egg white** before putting on the next. Repeat process, forming two additional stacks. Wrap waxed paper around blocks of dough. Chill. Remove from pan and unwrap. Cut into slices and bake as in △ Recipe.

Chocolate Banana Drops

Set out cookie sheets.

Melt (page 5) and set aside to cool
1 pkg. (6 oz.) semi-sweet chocolate pieces

Prepare and set aside
Cookie Topper (page 40)

Sift together and set aside
2¼ cups sifted all-purpose flour
2 teaspoons baking powder
¾ teaspoon salt
¼ teaspoon baking soda

Mash, rice or force through a food mill
2 to 3 all yellow or brown-flecked bananas (enough to make 1 cup mashed bananas)
Set aside.

Cream together until blended
⅔ cup shortening
1 teaspoon lemon extract
1 teaspoon vanilla extract
Add gradually, creaming until fluffy after each addition
1 cup sugar
Add in thirds, beating thoroughly after each addition
2 eggs, well beaten
Blend in melted chocolate. Stir in dry ingredients alternately with mashed bananas, adding dry ingredients in fourths, bananas in thirds.

Drop by teaspoonfuls about 1½ in. apart onto cookie sheets. Sprinkle with Cookie Topper.

Bake at 400°F 12 to 15 min.
About 5 doz. cookies

Frosted Shortbread Squares

Set out 15½x10½x1-in. pan.

Mix
    2 cups sifted all-purpose flour
    ½ cup firmly packed brown sugar
Cut in until mixture resembles coarse meal
    ¾ cup butter
Press firmly into ungreased pan.

Bake at 325°F 25 to 28 min.

Meanwhile, melt (page 5)
    **1 pkg. (6 oz.) semi-sweet chocolate
       pieces**
Spread quickly over hot, baked cookie dough. Sprinkle over top and gently press into chocolate
    ⅔ cup (about 3 oz.) chopped nuts
Cut into squares while warm.
70 1½-in. cookies

Luscious Chocolate Crispies

Generously grease cookie sheets.

Coarsely chop and set aside
    1¼ cups (about 5 oz.) nuts

Put into a saucepan and cook over low heat, stirring constantly, 3 min.
    ¾ cup firmly packed brown sugar
    ¼ cup butter
Remove from heat. Stir in chopped nuts and
    **½ pkg. (3 oz.) semi-sweet chocolate
       pieces**
Cool slightly (about 5 min.).

Add to chocolate mixture and mix well
    1 egg, well beaten
    1 teaspoon vanilla extract
    ¼ teaspoon almond extract

Drop by ½ teaspoonfuls onto cookie sheets.

Bake at 375°F 8 to 10 min. Let cookies cool until easy to remove. *About 3 doz. cookies*

Semi-Sweet Chocolate Favorites

    ▲ *Base Recipe*

Lightly grease 2 cookie sheets.

Chop and set aside
    1 cup (about 3¾ oz.) pecans

Sift together and set aside
    2½ cups sifted cake flour
    ¾ teaspoon baking soda
    ½ teaspoon salt

Cream together until blended
    1 cup shortening
    1 teaspoon vanilla extract
Add gradually, creaming until fluffy after each addition
    ¾ cup sugar
    ¾ cup firmly packed brown sugar
Add in thirds, beating well after each addition
    2 eggs, well beaten
Blend in
    2 tablespoons hot water

Add dry ingredients in fourths. Mix well after each addition. Stir in the chopped pecans and
    **1 pkg. (6 oz.) semi-sweet chocolate
       pieces**
Drop by teaspoonfuls onto cookie sheet about 2 in. apart.

Bake at 375°F 10 to 12 min.
About 4 doz. small cookies

—Semi-Sweet Chocolate Bars

Grease a 15½x10½x1-in. jelly roll pan.

Follow △ Recipe. Spread batter in pan and bake at 350°F 15 to 20 min. Cool completely; cut into 56 bars about 2x1½ in.

—Orange Semi-Sweet Cookies

Follow △ Recipe. Add 1 teaspoon grated **orange peel** (page 5) to the creamed shortening. Substitute **orange juice** for water.

—Semi-Sweet Chocolate Diamonds

Grease a 15½x10½x1-in. jelly roll pan.

Follow △ Recipe. Spread batter in pan and bake at 350° 15 to 20 min. Meanwhile, melt (page 7) a second package of **semi-sweet chocolate pieces** with 2 tablespoons **butter**; stir occasionally. Quickly spread evenly over baked cookies. If desired, sprinkle with chopped **pecans**. Cool completely; cut into diamond or wedge shapes.

Chip-Filled Oat Bars

Lightly grease 10x6x1½-in. pan.

Chop and set aside
    1 cup (about 3½ oz.) walnuts

Cream until shortening is softened
    ⅔ cup butter or margarine
    1 teaspoon vanilla extract
Add gradually, creaming until fluffy after each addition
    1 cup firmly packed brown sugar
Sift together and mix in
    1½ cups sifted all-purpose flour
    ¼ teaspoon salt
Mix in thoroughly
    1¼ cups uncooked rolled oats
Press one-half of this stiff, dry mixture into pan. Sprinkle with the chopped walnuts and
    **1 pkg. (6 oz.) semi-sweet chocolate
       pieces**
Cover with remaining mixture. Spread and press until flat and firm.

Bake at 375°F 35 to 40 min. Cut into 1x3-in. bars while warm. Cool in pan.
20 1x3-in. bars

Frosted Chocolate Nut Drops

▲ Base Recipe

Nut-filled drops are twice as good when chocolate is double featured.

Lightly grease cookie sheets.

For Cookies—Melt (page 5) and set aside to cool

4 oz. (4 sq.) chocolate

Coarsely chop and set aside

2 cups (7 oz.) black walnuts

Mix, sift together, and set aside

3 cups sifted all-purpose flour
½ teaspoon salt
½ teaspoon baking soda
½ teaspoon baking powder

Cream until shortening is softened

1 cup butter or margarine
2 teaspoons vanilla extract

Add gradually, creaming until fluffy after each addition

2 cups sugar

Add in thirds, beating thoroughly after each addition

3 eggs, well beaten

Stir in cooled chocolate.

Measure

1 cup sour milk

Alternately add dry ingredients in fourths, liquid in thirds, to creamed mixture. After each addition, beat only until smooth. Finally beat only until batter is smooth (do not overbeat). Blend in nuts. Drop by tablespoonfuls onto greased cookie sheets.

Bake at 350°F 12 to 15 min.

Remove cookies to cooling racks immediately and set aside to cool.

For Frosting—While cookies are cooling, melt (page 5) in double boiler top

3 to 4 oz. (3 to 4 sq.) chocolate
½ cup butter or margarine

Stir into the melted chocolate mixture

2⅔ cups sifted confectioners' sugar

Then stir in

1 egg
6 tablespoons water
2 teaspoons vanilla extract
⅛ teaspoon salt

Place the double boiler top in a bowl of ice and water. Beat with electric mixer about 5 min., or until frosting is of spreading consistency. If using a hand rotary beater, allow more beating time. Spread frosting on the cooled cookies, allowing about 1 tablespoon frosting for each cookie.

About 4 doz. cookies;
about 3 cups frosting

—Chocolate Fruit Drops

Follow △ Recipe. Replace 1 cup of nuts with an equal amount of **raisins** or chopped **dates**.

—Candy Chocolate Drops

Follow △ Recipe. Substitute 1½ cups **gumdrops**, cut in pieces, for nuts. Try many colored ones or use candy orange slices only.

Four-Stripers

Lightly grease cookie sheets.

Sift together and set aside

1¼ cups sifted all-purpose flour
¾ teaspoon baking soda
½ teaspoon baking powder
½ teaspoon salt

Cream until thoroughly blended

½ cup shortening
½ cup peanut butter
2 teaspoons vanilla extract

Add gradually, creaming until fluffy after each addition

1 cup firmly packed brown sugar

Beat in vigorously

1 egg, well beaten

Blend in dry ingredient in fourths. Mix well after each addition. Chill dough in refrigerator until firm. Pinch off small pieces and roll into balls. Place on cookie sheets. Melt (page 5)

½ pkg. (3 oz.) semi-sweet chocolate
pieces

Dip tines of fork into melted chocolate and flatten each cookie with chocolate-dipped fork.

Bake at 350°F 10 to 12 min.

4 to 5 doz. cookies

Fudge Oatmeal Squares

Lightly grease 8-in. square cake pan.

Coarsely chop

½ cup (about 2 oz.) nuts

Reserve 2 tablespoons of the chopped nuts for topping. Set aside.

Melt (page 5)

2 oz. (2 sq.) chocolate
⅓ cup butter or margarine

Remove from heat. Mix thoroughly in order

¼ cup light corn sirup
2 teaspoons vanilla extract
¼ teaspoon salt
⅔ cup sugar

Mix in the chopped nuts and

2 cups uncooked rolled oats

Spread the thick mixture into pan and sprinkle top with the reserved chopped nuts.

Bake at 400°F 12 min. Remove the soft, bubbling mixture from oven. Cut into 2x1-in. bars while warm. Cool thoroughly in pan. Store covered in cool place.

32 bars

Oatmeal Freckles

Illustrated on front cover

▲ Base Recipe

Lightly grease cookie sheets.

Chop and set aside
  ½ cup (about 2 oz.) nuts

Sift together into a bowl
  ¾ cup sifted all-purpose flour
  ½ cup sugar
  1 teaspoon cinnamon
  ½ teaspoon baking soda
  ½ teaspoon salt
Stir into sifted dry ingredients
  ½ cup firmly packed brown sugar

Add and beat together thoroughly (2 min. with electric mixer on medium speed)
  ½ cup shortening, softened
  1 egg, unbeaten
  3 tablespoons water
  1 teaspoon vanilla extract
Mix in the chopped nuts and
  1 pkg. (6 oz.) semi-sweet chocolate pieces
  1½ cups uncooked rolled oats
Drop by teaspoonfuls onto cookie sheets.

Bake at 375°F about 12 min.

About 6 doz. cookies

—Honey-Oatmeal Freckles

Follow △ Recipe. Omit brown sugar. Add ½ cup **honey** with the shortening. Decrease water to 1 tablespoon.

Fudge Brownies

▲ Base Recipe

Grease 8-in. square pan.

Melt (page 5) and set aside to cool
  2 oz. (2 sq.) chocolate

Sift together
  1 cup sifted cake flour
  ½ teaspoon baking powder
  ½ teaspoon salt
Chop, mix into dry ingredients and set aside
  1 cup (about 4 oz.) nuts

Cream together until blended
  ½ cup shortening
  ½ teaspoon vanilla extract
Add gradually, creaming until fluffy after each addition
  1 cup sugar
Add in thirds, beating thoroughly after each addition
  2 eggs, well beaten
Stir in chocolate. Blend in dry ingredients. Spread in pan.

Bake at 375°F 30 to 35 min. Cut into 2-in. squares while warm and cool in pan.

16 Fudge Brownies

—Peanut Butter Brownies

Follow △ Recipe. Cream ¼ cup **peanut butter** with the shortening. Use only ¼ cup (about 1¼ oz.) peanuts for nuts.

—Brownie Sandwiches

Follow △ Recipe. Substitute 3 oz. **semi-sweet chocolate pieces** for chocolate. Cool baked dough in pan; do not cut into squares.

For Filling—blend together 1 tablespoon softened **butter**, 1 cup sifted **confectioners' sugar**, 1 tablespoon **milk** and 2 or 3 drops **peppermint extract**. When brownies are cool, carefully remove from pan and cut into fourths. Split each fourth; set the top halves aside; spread filling over remaining lower halves. Place brownie tops over filling to form a sandwich. Cut into bar shapes.

—Coconut Toasties

Follow △ Recipe. While brownies bake, blend ½ cup moist, shredded **coconut**, 2 tablespoons softened **butter** or **margarine**. 2 tablespoons **top milk** or **cream** and ½ teaspoon **cinnamon**. Spread on baked brownies as soon as they are done. Place under broiler about 4 in. from source of heat for 2 min., or until topping bubbles. Watch closely to avoid scorching. Cool slightly. Cut into squares.

—Brownies à la Mode

Follow △ Recipe. Bake in greased 9-in. pie pan. Cut into six wedges; cool. Serve topped with **vanilla ice cream** and **chocolate sauce**.

Crispy Rolled Wafers

▲ Base Recipe

Set out cookie sheets.

Melt (page 5) and set aside to cool
  4 oz. (4 sq.) chocolate

Sift together three times and set aside
  2¼ cups sifted all-purpose flour
  1½ teaspoons baking powder
  ½ teaspoon baking soda
  ¼ teaspoon cinnamon

Cream together until blended
  ½ cup shortening
  1 tablespoon vanilla extract
Add gradually, creaming until fluffy after each addition
  1 cup sugar
Add in thirds, beating well after each addition
  2 eggs, well beaten
Blend in melted chocolate and
  1 tablespoon cream

Add sifted dry ingredients in fourths. Beat until smooth after each addition.

Roll dough thin on lightly floured surface. Cut with 3-in. cookie cutter or cut into squares. With spatula lift gently onto ungreased cookie sheet.

Bake at 400°F 5 to 7 min. Remove to cooling rack at once.

4 doz. 3-in. wafers

—Crumbs for Cookie Crust

Follow △ Recipe. Roll dough thin on waxed paper cut to fit cookie sheet. Lift paper to cookie sheet; invert onto cookie sheet and gently remove paper from dough. Bake at 400°F 5 to 7 min. Remove to cooling rack at once. When cool, roll into crumbs and store in covered jar or container. Use for **Frosty Cookie Crumb Pie** (page 30).

About 3¼ cups crumbs

—Mint-Filled Wafers

Follow △ Recipe. Place an **after-dinner mint pattie** on an unbaked cookie cut slightly larger than mint. Cover with another unbaked cookie. Press edges together with tines of a fork. Bake at 400°F 5 to 7 min. Remove to cooling rack at once.

—Teatime Temptations

Follow △ Recipe. Use small, fancy-shape cookie cutter. Spread baked wafers with filling and press pairs together.

For Filling—Work together until smooth and blended thoroughly 1 pkg. (3 oz.) **cream cheese**, 2¼ cups sifted **confectioners' sugar**, 3 tablespoons **orange juice** and 1 teaspoon grated **orange peel** (page 5).

Marbled Brownies

The aristocrat of brownies—a perfect match for iced coffee.

Cream until softened
   1½ tablespoons butter or margarine
Add gradually, creaming until fluffy after each addition
   3 tablespoons sugar
Blend in, in order, and set aside
   2 teaspoons cornstarch
   ⅔ cup dry cottage cheese
   1 egg, well beaten
   1 tablespoon milk
   ½ teaspoon vanilla extract
   ⅛ teaspoon salt
Prepare
   Fudge Brownies (page 24; omit nuts)
Grease 9-in. sq. pan and spread one-half of brownie dough in bottom of pan. Spread cheese mixture over chocolate layer. Spread remaining half of dough over cheese. Draw spoon through layers until marbled effect is produced.

Bake at 375°F 40 to 45 min. or until wooden pick inserted in center comes out clean. Cool in pan and cut into squares.

16 brownies

Pecan-Chocolate Miniatures

Line with paper baking cups or lightly grease bottoms of 3 doz. 1¾-in. muffin pan wells.

Melt (page 5) together, and set aside to cool
   1 oz. (1 sq.) chocolate
   2 tablespoons butter or margarine

Finely chop and set aside
   1 cup (about 3¾ oz.) pecans

Sift together and set aside
   ⅓ cup sifted all-purpose flour
   ¼ teaspoon baking soda
   ¼ teaspoon salt
Beat until thick and piled softly
   2 eggs
Add gradually, beating thoroughly after each addition
   ½ cup firmly packed brown sugar
Blend in cooled chocolate mixture and
   2 tablespoons milk
   ½ teaspoon vanilla extract
Add dry ingredients and quickly blend in. Stir in the chopped pecans. Spoon into muffin wells filling wells one-half to two-thirds full.

Bake at 375°F 10 to 12 min., or until tops spring back when touched lightly. Remove from muffin wells and place on cooling rack.

3 doz. miniature cupcakes

Cocoa Drops

▲ *Base Recipe*

Lightly grease cookie sheets.

Sift together and set aside
   1½ cups sifted cake flour
   ¾ cup cocoa
   ¼ teaspoon salt

Cream together until shortening is softened
   1 cup butter or margarine
   1 teaspoon vanilla extract
Add gradually, creaming until fluffy after each addition
   ¾ cup sugar
Add in thirds, beating thoroughly after each addition
   2 eggs, well beaten
Stir in dry ingredients in fourths. Mix well after each addition. Drop by teaspoonfuls about 2 in. apart onto the cookie sheets.

Bake at 375°F 12 to 15 min.

About 7 doz. wafers

—Coconut Chocolate Wafers

Follow △ Recipe. Use **Dutch process cocoa**. Chop ⅔ cup moist, shredded **coconut** extremely fine and blend in after dry ingredients.

Cocoa Almond Bars Supreme

Lightly grease 8x8x2-in. pan.

Blanch, toast (page 5), chop coarsely and set aside
    1 cup (about 5½ oz.) almonds

Sift together and set aside
    ⅔ cup sifted all-purpose flour
    ⅓ cup Dutch process cocoa
    ½ teaspoon baking powder
    ¼ teaspoon salt

Cream until thoroughly blended
    ½ cup shortening
    ¼ cup almond paste
    1½ teaspoons vanilla extract
    ½ teaspoon almond extract
Add gradually, creaming until fluffy after each addition
    ¾ cup sugar

Beat vigorously
    1 egg
    1 egg yolk
Add in thirds to creamed mixture, beating thoroughly after each addition. Blend in the dry ingredients in fourths. Mix well after each addition. Stir in ½ cup of the chopped almonds (reserve other ½ cup). Mix thoroughly. Spread in pan and set aside.

Beat until frothy
    1 egg white
    ¼ teaspoon cream of tartar
Add gradually and beat well after each addition
    ¼ cup sugar
Continue beating until stiff peaks are formed. Fold (page 7) in reserved almonds. Spread mixture over batter in pan.

Bake at 350°F 35 to 40 min., or until meringue is lightly browned and wooden pick inserted in center of baked dough comes out clean. Cut into 2x1-in. bars when thoroughly cooled.
2½ doz. cookies

Cocoa Dream Bars

Set out 11x7x1½-in. cake pan.

Mix together
    1 cup sifted all-purpose flour
    ½ cup cocoa
    ¼ cup firmly packed brown sugar
    ¼ teaspoon salt
Blend in with pastry blender until a soft dough is formed
    ½ cup butter
Turn into the pan and press evenly and firmly to cover bottom.

Bake at 375°F 10 min. Cool slightly.

Meanwhile, coarsely chop and set aside
    1 cup (about 4 oz.) nuts
Set out
    1½ cups (about 4 oz.) flaked coconut

Beat slightly
    2 eggs
Beat in until very thick
    1 cup sugar
    1 teaspoon vanilla extract

Mix together thoroughly the chopped nuts, coconut and
    3 tablespoons all-purpose flour
    ½ teaspoon salt
    1 teaspoon baking powder
Combine egg and flour mixtures and blend well; spread over the partially cooled crust.

Bake at 350°F 25 to 30 min. Cut into bars while warm. Cool thoroughly in pan.
About 20 bars

Chocolate Macaroons

  ▲ *Base Recipe*

Cover the bottom of a cookie sheet with unglazed paper.

Melt (page 5) and set aside to cool
    1½ oz. (1½ sq.) chocolate

Beat until frothy
    2 egg whites
Add and beat slightly
    1 teaspoon vanilla extract
    ¼ teaspoon salt
Add, one tablespoon at a time, beating well after each addition and finally beating until very stiff peaks are formed
    1 cup sugar
Fold (page 5) in chocolate and
    1½ cups (4 to 5 oz.) moist, shredded or flaked coconut

Drop by teaspoonfuls onto unglazed paper. Keep macaroons small and uniform.

Bake at 350°F 20 to 25 min.
15 to 20 small macaroons

—Crunchy Nut Macaroons

Follow △ Recipe. Decrease coconut to ½ cup. Add 1 cup **cereal** such as corn or wheat flakes and ¼ cup (about 1 oz.) chopped **nuts**.

—Filbert Sweetstuffs

Follow △ Recipe. Substitute chopped **filberts** for coconut.

Pies

Plain Pastry for 1-Crust Pie

▲ Base Recipe

Set out 8- or 9-in. pie pan.

Sift together
     1 cup sifted all-purpose flour
     ½ teaspoon salt
Cut in with pastry blender or two knives until pieces are size of small peas
     ⅓ cup lard, hydrogenated vegetable shortening or all-purpose shortening
Sprinkle gradually over mixture, 1 teaspoon at a time, about
     2½ tablespoons cold water
Mix lightly with fork after each addition. Add only enough water to hold pastry together. Work quickly; do not overhandle. Shape into a ball and flatten on a lightly floured surface. Lightly flour rolling pin. Roll from center to edge into a round about ⅛ in. thick and about 1 in. larger than over-all size of pan. With knife or spatula, loosen pastry from surface wherever sticking occurs; lift pastry slightly and sprinkle flour underneath.

Loosen one half from board with spatula and fold over other half. Loosen remaining part and fold in quarters. Gently lay pastry in pan and unfold, fitting it to the pan so that it is not stretched.

Trim edge with scissors or sharp knife to overlap ½ in. Fold under extra pastry at edge, and flute (page 5) with fingers or fork. Prick bottom and sides of shell thoroughly with a fork. (Omit pricking if filling is to be baked in shell.) Bake at 450°F 10 to 15 min., or until light, golden brown. Set on cooling rack to cool.
One 8- or 9-in. pastry shell

For 10-inch Pastry Shell—Increase flour to 1⅓ cups, shortening to ½ cup, salt to ¾ teaspoon and water to about 3 tablespoons.

—Pastry for Little Pies and Tarts

Double △ Recipe. Roll pastry ⅛ in. thick. Cut about ½ in. larger than over-all size of tart or small pie pans. Fit rounds into pans without stretching, carefully fold extra pastry under at edges and press together with a fork, or flute (page 5). Prick bottom and sides of shell thoroughly with fork. (Omit pricking if filling is to be baked in shell.)

Bake at 450°F 8 to 10 min, or until light, golden brown. Cool and carefully remove from pans.
6 little (6-in.) pies, 12 3-in. tarts, or 18 1½-in. tarts

—Braided Edge

Prepare Plain Pastry for 1-Crust Pie but do not flute edge. Set aside.

For Braided Edge Only—Follow △ Recipe using ½ cup sifted flour, 3 tablespoons shortening, ¼ teaspoon salt and about 1½ tablespoons water. Roll pastry 14 in. long and ⅛ in. thick. Cut nine lengthwise strips, ¼ in. wide. With strips on board, carefully braid three strips loosely; repeat twice. Brush rim of pastry with water and place three braids on rim. Join by overlapping and pressing ends together.

Angel Chocolate Pie

Lightly grease a 9-in. piepan.

Beat in a large bowl with a rotary beater until frothy
     4 egg whites
Add
     ½ teaspoon cream of tartar
     ⅛ teaspoon salt
Add gradually, beating well after each addition
     1 cup sugar
Continue beating until very stiff peaks are formed. Spread a 1-in. layer of meringue on bottom of pie pan. Pile remaining meringue around edge of pan and swirl with spatula to form sides of shell.

Bake the meringue shell at 275°F for 1½ hrs. Turn off oven heat and leave meringue in oven 1 hr. (Do not open oven door at any time.) Remove meringue shell from the oven and place on a cooling rack until completely cooled. Gently remove the shell from pie pan and if not used immediately store it in an airtight container so meringue will not absorb moisture and become soft. It should be crisp, dry and have a very fine texture.

Prepare and chill thoroughly
     Filling for Chocolate Cream Pie or any variation (page 28)
Spoon chilled filling into meringue shell.
6 to 8 servings

Banana Chocolate-Mallow Pie

▲ Base Recipe

Set a rotary beater and a bowl in refrigerator to chill.

Prepare and bake in an 8-in. pie pan
**Plain Pastry for 1-Crust Pie (page 27)
or Frosty Cookie Crumb crust or
Frosty Graham Cracker crust
(page 30)**
Set aside on cooling rack to cool.

Combine in top of double boiler
**16 (about 4 oz.) marshmallows
½ cup milk
1 oz. (1 sq.) chocolate, cut in pieces**
Heat over simmering water until marshmallows and chocolate are melted, stirring occasionally. Remove from heat; let stand until cool but not set.

Meanwhile, arrange in an even layer over bottom of baked pie shell
**3 all-yellow or brown-flecked
bananas, cut in ¼-in. slices**

Using chilled rotary beater and bowl, beat until of medium consistency (piles softly)
1 cup chilled whipping cream
Fold (page 5) whipped cream into the cooled marshmallow mixture. Turn filling into pie shell and spread evenly over bananas. Put pie into refrigerator and chill until set (about 1½ to 2 hrs.).

6 servings

—Banana Cocoa-Mallow Pie

Follow △ Recipe. Omit grated chocolate. Combine ¼ cup cocoa and 2 tablespoons water; cook over low heat, stirring constantly, until mixture is smooth. Add to hot marshmallow mixture and blend well.

De Luxe Caramel Pecan Pie

Prepare but do not bake in an 8-in. pie pan
Plain Pastry for 1-Crust Pie (page 27)
Set aside.

Combine
**1 cup milk
2 egg yolks, slightly beaten
2 tablespoons butter or margarine,
melted
1 teaspoon vanilla extract**

Stir in a mixture of
**½ cup sugar
½ cup firmly packed brown sugar
2 tablespoons all-purpose flour**
Set aside.

Beat until rounded peaks are formed
2 egg whites
Fold (page 5) gently into egg yolk mixture. Pour into pie shell.

Bake at 450°F 10 min. Quickly reduce heat to 350°F and bake 25 to 30 min. longer or until a silver knife inserted halfway between center and edge of filling comes out clean.

Top cooled pie with Glossy Chocolate Frosting (page 18) and pecan halves.

6 servings

Chocolate Cream Pie

▲ Base Recipe

Prepare and bake in an 8-in. pie pan
Plain Pastry for 1-Crust Pie (page 27)
Set aside on cooling rack to cool.

Heat in double boiler top until milk is scalded (page 6) and chocolate is melted
**1½ cups milk
2 oz. (2 sq.) chocolate**

Meanwhile, mix thoroughly in saucepan
**⅔ cup sugar
¼ cup all-purpose flour
¼ teaspoon salt**
Blend dry ingredients with
½ cup cold milk
Stir in chocolate-milk mixture. Wash double boiler top to remove scum. Stirring gently and constantly, bring rapidly to boiling over direct heat and cook for 3 min. Pour into double boiler top and place over simmering water. Cover and cook about 5 to 7 min., stirring occasionally. Remove cover and vigorously stir about 3 tablespoons of this hot mixture into
3 egg yolks, slightly beaten
Immediately blend into mixture in double boiler. Cook over simmering water 3 to 5 min. Stir slowly to keep mixture cooking evenly. Remove from heat. Stir in
**2 tablespoons butter or margarine
2 teaspoons vanilla extract**
Cover, cool and chill in refrigerator. Pour into cooled pie shell. Top with mounds of **whipped cream** just before serving. Arrange **semi-sweet chocolate pieces** on each mound.

6 servings

—Cocoa Cream Pie

Follow △ Recipe. Substitute ½ cup **cocoa** for chocolate. Mix cocoa with dry ingredients.

—Mocha Chocolate Cream Pie

Follow △ Recipe. Substitute 1 cup **double-strength coffee beverage** for 1 cup milk.

—Chocolate Cream Pudding

Follow △ Recipe. Omit pie shell. Pour hot filling into 4 individual serving dishes. When cool, serve with **cream**.

Honey-Chocolate Pie

Prepare and bake in a 9-in. pie pan
        Plain Pastry for 1-Crust Pie (page 27)
Set aside on cooling rack to cool.

Heat in double boiler top until milk is scalded (page 6) and chocolate melted
        2 cups milk
        2 oz. (2 sq.) chocolate

Meanwhile, combine in saucepan
        ⅓ cup sifted all-purpose flour
        ½ teaspoon salt
Add, stirring well, a mixture of
        ½ cup cold milk
        ½ cup honey
Gradually stir in scalded milk and chocolate. Wash double boiler top to remove scum. Stirring gently and constantly, bring starch mixture to boiling over direct heat and cook for 3 min. Pour into double boiler top and place over simmering water. Cover and cook 5 to 7 min., stirring occasionally. Vigorously stir about 3 tablespoons hot mixture into
        3 egg yolks, slightly beaten
Immediately blend into mixture in double boiler. Cook over simmering water 3 to 5 min. Stir slowly to keep mixture cooking evenly. Remove from heat. Stir in
        2 tablespoons butter or margarine
        1 teaspoon vanilla extract
Cover and cool. Chill in refrigerator.

Prepare a meringue by beating in a bowl until frothy
        3 egg whites
        ⅛ teaspoon salt
Add gradually and beat well after each addition, finally beating until very stiff peaks are formed
        6 tablespoons sugar

Pour cooled filling into cooled pie shell; pile meringue onto filling, being sure to seal meringue to crust.

Bake at 350°F 10 to 15 min., or until meringue is delicately browned. Cool.

Melt (page 5) and set aside to cool
        ½ oz. (½ sq.) chocolate
Streak cooled meringue with melted chocolate.
6 servings

Velvet Chocolate Pie

   ▲ *Base Recipe*
Prepare and bake in a 10-in. pie pan
        Plain Pastry for 1-Crust Pie (page 27)
Set aside on cooling rack to cool.

Meanwhile, mix thoroughly in top of a double boiler
        1 env. unflavored gelatin
        ¼ cup sugar
        ⅛ teaspoon salt
Beat together in a bowl until well blended
        3 egg yolks
        1¾ cups milk
Blend into the gelatin mixture in top of the double boiler. Set over boiling water in the bottom of double boiler and cook, stirring occasionally, about 5 min., or until gelatin is completely dissolved. Remove from heat and stir in until chocolate is melted
        1 pkg. (6 oz.) semi-sweet chocolate
            pieces
        1 teaspoon vanilla extract

Chill in refrigerator or in a pan of ice and water until mixture mounds slightly when dropped from a spoon. (If mixture is placed over ice and water, stir frequently; if placed in refrigerator, stir occasionally.)

When the mixture begins to thicken, beat until frothy
        3 egg whites
Add and continue to beat until thoroughly blended
        ¼ teaspoon cream of tartar
Add gradually, beating well after each addition
        ½ cup sugar
Continue beating until very stiff peaks are formed. Fold (page 5) beaten egg whites into cooled gelatin mixture. Pour into baked pie shell and chill in refrigerator until filling is set (about 2 hrs.).
6 to 8 servings

—Chocolate Velvet Tarts

Follow △ Recipe. Prepare and bake 24 to 30 1½ in. tarts (1½ times recipe, page 27). Fill each cooled tart shell with about 2½ tablespoons filling. Top with sweetened **whipped cream** (page 7) and one **semi-sweet chocolate piece** for each tart.

Cocoa Chiffon Pie

▲ *Base Recipe*

Prepare and bake in an 8-in. pie pan
   Plain Pastry for 1-Crust Pie (page 27)
Set aside on cooling rack to cool.

Meanwhile, mix thoroughly in top of a double boiler
   1 env. unflavored gelatin
   ⅓ cup sugar
   ⅓ cup cocoa
   ¼ teaspoon salt
Beat together in a bowl until thoroughly blended
   4 egg yolks
   1 cup milk

Blend into the gelatin mixture in top of the double boiler. Set over boiling water in the bottom of double boiler and cook, stirring occasionally, about 5 min. or until gelatin is completely dissolved.
Blend in
   1 teaspoon vanilla extract
Chill in refrigerator or in a pan of ice and water until mixture mounds slightly when dropped from a spoon. (If mixture is placed over ice and water, stir frequently; if placed in refrigerator, stir occasionally.)

When mixture begins to thicken, beat until frothy
   4 egg whites
Add gradually, beating well after each addition
   ⅓ cup sugar
Continue to beat until very stiff peaks are formed. Gently fold (page 5) a small amount of the beaten egg whites into chilled chocolate mixture. Spoon about one half of the chocolate mixture over the remaining egg whites and fold until blended. Fold in remaining chocolate mixture. Turn into pie shell and chill in refrigerator until set.

Serve topped with sweetened **whipped cream** (page 6). If desired, sprinkle lightly over whipped cream topping about ¼ cup toasted shredded or flaked **coconut** or finely chopped **pecans** or **chocolate cookie crumbs**.

6 servings

—Chocolate Chiffon Pie

Follow △ Recipe. Substitute 2 oz. (2 sq.) **chocolate**, grated for cocoa. Increase each sugar measurement to ½ cup.

—Brazil Nut Chiffon Pie

Follow △ Recipe using cocoa or chocolate. Fold in ½ cup **whipping cream**, whipped, before turning into pie shell. Top with shaved, curled **Brazil nuts**.

Frosty Cookie Crumb Pie

▲ *Base Recipe*

Set out 8- or 9-in. pie pan.

Blend
   1⅓ cups Crumbs for Cookie Crust
      (page 25)
   ¼ cup softened butter or margarine
Using back of a spoon, press firmly on bottom and sides of the pan.

Bake at 325°F 10 min. Cool thoroughly before adding filling.

Fill crust with
   1 qt. vanilla ice cream
Top with grated chocolate, nuts, coconut, crushed peppermint stick candy or any chocolate sauce. Serve at once or store in freezing compartment of refrigerator.

6 servings

—Frosty Graham Cracker Pie

Follow △ Recipe. Substitute **graham cracker crumbs** (about 16 to 18 crackers) for the cookie crumbs. Blend in ¼ cup **sugar**, 4 oz. finely chopped **milk or semi-sweet chocolate** and ½ teaspoon **cinnamon**.

Black Bottom Pie

▲ *Base Recipe*

A queen of pies, handsome and rich.

Prepare and bake in a 10-in. pie pan
   Plain Pastry for 1-Crust Pie with
      Braided Edge (page 27)
Set aside on cooling rack to cool.

Melt (page 5) and set aside to cool
   1½ oz. (1½ sq.) chocolate

Pour into a small cup or custard cup
   ¼ cup cold water
Sprinkle evenly over the water
   1 env. unflavored gelatin
Let stand until softened.

For Custard Filling—Beat slightly and set aside
   4 egg yolks

Scald (page 6) in double boiler top
   1½ cups milk

Meanwhile, blend thoroughly in a heavy saucepan
   ½ cup sugar
   4 teaspoons cornstarch
Add and blend in well
   ½ cup cold milk

Stir hot milk into cornstarch mixture. Wash double boiler top to remove scum. Bring rapidly to boiling over direct heat, stirring gently and constantly. Cook 3 min. Pour into double boiler top.

Vigorously stir about 3 tablespoons of hot mixture into egg yolks. Immediately blend into cooked mixture, stirring constantly. Cook over simmering water 3 to 5 min., until mixture thickens, or coats a silver spoon. Remove from heat. Remove 1 cup cooked filling mixture from double boiler and set aside.

Add softened gelatin to mixture in double boiler. Stir until gelatin is completely dissolved. Set aside. Cool until the mixture sets slightly. If it becomes too stiff upon standing, soften over simmering water. Cool again.

For Chocolate Filling—Stir melted chocolate into the 1 cup of reserved filling with
> **2 teaspoons vanilla extract**

Cool completely. Pour into pie shell and spread evenly over bottom. Chill until set.

To Complete Pie—Meanwhile, beat until frothy
> **4 egg whites**
> **¼ teaspoon salt**

Add and continue to beat egg whites slightly
> **¼ teaspoon cream of tartar**

Add gradually, beating well after each addition
> **½ cup sugar**

Continue beating until very stiff peaks are formed. Fold (page 5) into cooled plain filling. Blend in
> **1 tablespoon rum extract**

Pour over set chocolate filling in pie shell. Chill until firm.

Set a rotary beater and bowl in refrigerator to chill.

When ready to serve, use chilled bowl and beater and whip until cream stands in peaks when beater is slowly lifted upright
> **1 cup chilled whipping cream**

Spread on pie. Top with chocolate curls made by pulling across a shredder
> **½ oz. (½ sq.) chocolate**

Chill until ready to serve.

6 to 8 servings

—Black Bottom Pie II

Follow △ Recipe. Omit chocolate. Add vanilla extract after removing filling from heat. While pie shell is still warm, place 2 or 3 **milk chocolate bars**, broken in pieces, or 1 pkg. (6 oz.) **semi-sweet chocolate pieces** in shell. When cool and set, pour filling mixture over chocolate. Chill. Top as directed.

Desserts

Double-Rich Fudge Pudding

This dessert separates into a rich cake with a creamy chocolate sauce underneath.

Grease a deep 8-in. round cake pan.

Sift together into a bowl and set aside
- **1¼ cups sifted cake flour**
- **¾ cup sugar**
- **½ teaspoon baking soda**
- **¼ teaspoon salt**

Melt (page 5) and set aside
- **1 oz. (1 sq.) chocolate**
- **2 tablespoons butter or margarine**

Pour into a measuring cup
- **2 tablespoons vinegar**

Add
- **6 tablespoons milk (or enough to make ½ cup liquid)**

Stir milk-vinegar mixture (soured milk) into melted chocolate mixture with
- **1 teaspoon vanilla extract**

Add chocolate-milk mixture, all at once, to dry ingredients. Stir until thoroughly blended. Add
- **1 cup (3¾ oz.) salted pecan halves**

Blend just until pecan halves are evenly distributed. Turn batter into pan. Sprinkle over batter and set aside
- **1 cup firmly packed brown sugar**

Combine
- **1½ cups boiling water**
- **2 oz. (2 sq.) chocolate**

Stir until chocolate is melted and thoroughly blended with water. Pour over top of batter.

Bake pudding at 350°F 45 to 50 min. Serve warm with **heavy cream, whipped cream** or **vanilla ice cream.**

8 to 10 servings

—Double Fudge Pudding

Follow △ Recipe. Substitute 2 teaspoons **baking powder** for baking soda. Omit vinegar and increase milk to ½ cup. Omit salted pecan halves. Reduce brown sugar to ½ cup and combine with it ½ cup **granulated sugar** and 2 tablespoons **cocoa.** Omit chocolate (which is poured over top) and reduce boiling water to 1 cup. Bake and serve as in △ Recipe.

—Mocha Fudge Pudding

Follow △ Recipe or Double Fudge Pudding. Add 2 teaspoons **concentrated soluble coffee** with the brown sugar. Batter may be spooned into individual, heat-resistant custard cups, sprinkled with topping and the hot water poured over each pudding.

Chocolate-Topped Meringue

Sift into top of double boiler
- **½ cup sugar**
- **¼ cup cocoa**
- **¼ teaspoon salt**

Add and stir until smooth
- **¾ cup milk**

Continue stirring and add
- **1 cup milk**

Place over direct heat. Stir constantly and gently while bringing rapidly to boiling. Place over simmering water.

Vigorously stir about 3 tablespoons of hot mixture into
- **3 egg yolks, slightly beaten**

Immediately blend egg yolk mixture into hot mixture in double boiler. Stir constantly and rapidly. Cook over simmering water until mixture coats a silver spoon. Remove from heat. Stir in
- **1 tablespoon butter**
- **2 teaspoons vanilla extract**

Pour into bowl. Cover. Chill in refrigerator.

Before serving, prepare a meringue by beating until frothy
- **3 egg whites**
- **⅛ teaspoon salt**

Add gradually and beat well after each addition
- **⅓ cup sugar**

Continue beating until very stiff peaks are formed. Heap meringue lightly into **serving dishes.** Top with chilled chocolate custard.

5 servings

Chocolate Fluff Pudding

▲ *Base Recipe*

Melt (page 5)
- **2 oz. (2 sq.) chocolate**

Add
- **1¼ cups (14-oz. can) sweetened condensed milk**

Stir over rapidly boiling water until mixture thickens. Remove from heat. Stir in
- **½ cup water**
- **½ teaspoon almond extract**

Let cool for about 5 min.

Beat until rounded peaks are formed
- **2 egg whites**

Fold (page 5) egg whites into chocolate mixture. Fill sherbet glasses. Chill in refrigerator.

6 servings

Note: This pudding can be used as a filling for an 8-in. pie shell.

—Sherry Fluff Pudding

Follow △ Recipe. Fold in 1 teaspoon **sherry extract** with beaten egg whites.

Pots de Crème Chocolat

▲ *Base Recipe*

Choice custard, soft or baked, a memorable chocolate treat of historic importance.

Set out 6 heat-resistant custard cups.

Heat over simmering water until milk or cream is scalded (page 6) and chocolate melted
> **3 cups milk or cream**
> **2½ oz. (2½ sq.) chocolate**
Set aside.

Beat slightly
> **5 egg yolks**
Stir in
> **¾ cup sugar**
Add hot chocolate mixture slowly, stirring vigorously and constantly. Strain. Blend in
> **1 tablespoon vanilla extract**
Pour into custard cups. Set in oven in water bath (page 6).

Bake at 325°F 30 to 40 min., or until a silver knife inserted in custard comes out clean.

6 servings

—Crème au Chocolat

Follow △ Recipe. Pour strained custard mixture into top of double boiler and continue to cook over simmering water, stirring constantly and rapidly, until mixture coats a silver spoon. Remove from heat at once. Cool. Blend in vanilla extract. Pour into custard cups or serving dish. Mixture will be the consistency of whipping cream. Chill in refrigerator. Serve with sweetened **whipped cream** (page 6).

Dessert Superb

Grease bottom of 15½x10½x1-in. jelly roll pan; line bottom with waxed paper allowing paper to extend about 1 in. beyond ends of pan; grease paper.

Put into top of a double boiler
> **½ lb. sweet chocolate (in pieces)**
> **7 tablespoons double-strength coffee beverage**
Set over simmering water until chocolate is melted. Remove from water and set aside to cool.

Beat with an electric beater until very thick
> **½ cup (6 or 7) egg yolks**
> **¾ cup sugar**
> **1 teaspoon vanilla extract**
Set aside.

Beat until frothy using a clean beater
> **1 cup (7 or 8) egg whites**
> **¼ teaspoon salt**
Add gradually, beating until stiff peaks form
> **¼ cup sugar**

Stir the cooled chocolate and blend into egg yolk mixture. Gently stir in egg whites. Turn into the lined pan; spread evenly.

Bake at 350°F 20 min. Set on a cooling rack until slightly cool. Sift over clean towel
> **2 tablespoons Dutch process cocoa**
Cut around edge of pan to loosen dessert; turn out onto the towel. Carefully remove paper. If desired, let stand about 30 min. to absorb cocoa flavor. Cover with waxed paper until ready to serve. Just before serving, whip until stiff
> **1 cup chilled whipping cream**
Blend in
> **3 tablespoons sifted confectioners' sugar**
> **1 teaspoon vanilla extract**
Cut dessert into 16 squares. Transfer 8 to plates. Spoon whipped cream onto each. Top with remaining squares, cocoa-side up.

8 servings

Chocolate Crinkle Cups

Twelve muffin pan wells and 12 2-in. paper baking cups will be needed.

Melt over hot (not simmering) water
> **1 pkg. (12 oz.) semi-sweet chocolate pieces**
Remove from heat and stir. With back of teaspoon or small spatula, spread chocolate on inside of baking cups. Set in muffin pan wells. Place in refrigerator and chill until firm (about 1 hr.). Carefully peel off paper cups. Fill with **pudding**, whipped **gelatin**, **candies**, **sherbet**, or **ice cream**. Serve at once.

12 crinkle cups

Chocolate Fondue

Grease bottom of shallow 2-qt. baking dish.

Heat in a large heavy saucepan, stirring frequently until chocolate is melted
> **2 cups milk**
> **4 oz. (4 sq.) chocolate**
Stir in
> **1¼ cups fine soft bread crumbs (4 slices bread, crusts removed)**
> **2 tablespoons butter or margarine**
> **1 cup sugar**
> **½ teaspoon salt**
Blend a few tablespoons of the mixture into
> **6 egg yolks, slightly beaten**
Return to the mixture in saucepan and blend well. Stir in
> **4 to 6 teaspoons vanilla extract**
Beat until rounded peaks are formed
> **6 egg whites**
Fold (page 5) into the chocolate mixture. Turn mixture into baking dish.

Place in oven in water bath (page 6) and bake at 350°F about 40 min., or until a silver knife inserted halfway between center and edge comes out clean. Lightly sift over top of fondue
> **Dutch process cocoa**
Serve warm.

8 servings

Minted Chocolate Fluff

▲ *Base Recipe*

Combine in top of double boiler
   1 pkg. (6 oz.) semi-sweet chocolate pieces
   1 cup milk
Set over hot (not simmering) water and heat, stirring occasionally, until chocolate is melted.

Meanwhile, pour into a small bowl or cup
   ¼ cup cold water
Sprinkle evenly over the water

   1½ teaspoons unflavored gelatin
Let stand to soften.

Meanwhile, beat until thick and lemon-colored
   4 egg yolks
Pour chocolate mixture slowly into beaten egg yolks, stirring constantly. Return to top of double boiler and cook, stirring constantly, over simmering water 5 min. Remove from heat; add softened gelatin, stirring until gelatin is completely dissolved. Set aside to cool.

Beat until frothy
   4 egg whites
Add gradually, beating well after each addition
   ½ cup sugar
Beat until very stiff peaks are formed. Fold (page 5) beaten egg whites into chocolate mixture with
   1 teaspoon vanilla extract
   ½ teaspoon peppermint extract
Pour into sherbet glasses. Chill in refrigerator.
About 6 servings

—Minted Chocolate Cream Fluff

Follow △ Recipe. Omit egg whites. Using chilled bowl and beater whip 1 cup chilled **whipping cream** until of medium consistency (piles softly). Beat in ½ cup **sugar**. Fold into chocolate mixture with flavoring extracts.

Top o' Range Date-Fudge Pudding

Set out heavy 3-qt. saucepan or skillet having tight-fitting cover.

Melt (page 5) and set aside to cool
   2 oz. (2 sq.) chocolate

Chop and set aside
   ½ cup (about 2 oz.) nuts

Cut in pieces (page 5) and set aside
   ½ cup pitted dates

Sift together and set aside
   1 cup sifted all-purpose flour
   2½ teaspoons baking powder
   1½ teaspoons cinnamon
   ½ teaspoon salt

Cream together until thoroughly blended
   ⅓ cup shortening
   1 teaspoon vanilla extract

Add gradually, creaming until fluffy after each addition
   ¼ cup sugar
Blend in the melted chocolate. Add dry ingredients alternately with
   ½ cup milk
Blend well after each addition. Fold (page 5) nuts and dates into batter and set aside.

Bring to boiling in the saucepan, stirring until chocolate is melted, a mixture of
   2 cups water
   ½ cup sugar
   1 oz. (1 sq.) chocolate
   1 teaspoon vanilla extract
Drop heaping tablespoonfuls of batter into hot chocolate mixture. Cover tightly and cook over low heat 35 to 40 min. Serve immediately.
6 servings

Chocolate Soufflé

Butter the bottom and sides of a 1½-qt. soufflé dish or casserole; sprinkle lightly with sugar.

Heat in top of double boiler over simmering water until chocolate is melted and milk is scalded (page 6)
   2 oz. (2 sq.) chocolate
   ½ cup milk
Beat with rotary beater until smooth; set aside.

Combine in a bowl
   ⅓ cup all-purpose flour
   ¼ cup sugar
   ¼ teaspoon salt
Gradually add, stirring until blended
   ½ cup milk
Stir into mixture in double boiler. Cook over boiling water, stirring until thick and smooth. Remove from water. Beat with hand rotary or electric beater about 1 min.

Beat until thick and lemon colored
   4 egg yolks
Add hot mixture gradually while beating constantly. Add and continue beating until smooth
   1 tablespoon vanilla extract
Set aside.

Beat until frothy
   4 egg whites
Add gradually, beating until stiff peaks form
   ¼ cup sugar
Gently fold (page 5) one-fourth of the chocolate mixture at a time into egg whites until well blended after each addition. Turn into the soufflé dish.

Bake at 425°F about 25 min., or until silver knife inserted halfway between center and edge comes out clean. Serve immediately with sweetened whipped cream (page 6).
6 servings

Chocalinda

Set out an 8-in. square pan.

Sliver and set aside
   **½ cup (3 oz.) blanched, toasted and
       salted almonds (page 5)**

Finely crush
   **8 graham crackers (about ⅔ cup,
       crushed)**
Sprinkle the crushed graham crackers evenly
over bottom of pan.

Put into a bowl
   2 cups sifted confectioners' sugar
   ½ cup cocoa
   ½ cup butter or margarine, softened
   2 eggs
   1 teaspoon vanilla extract
Beat with electric mixer until smooth, creamy,
light in color and mixture stands in peaks. Do
not overbeat. Using spoon or rubber spatula
take portions of mixture and place carefully
in each corner and in middle of graham cracker
crumb-lined pan. Gently spread mixture to
cover entire pan. Sprinkle the almonds over
the mixture. Using back of spoon, gently
press almonds onto mixture. Chill in refrigerator 12 hrs. Serve thoroughly chilled.

8 servings

Toffee Dessert

▲ *Base Recipe*

Butter an 8-in. square pan.

Melt (page 5) and set aside to cool
   2 oz. (2 sq.) chocolate

Crush to fine crumbs
   ¼ lb. vanilla wafers
Blend in
   1 cup (about 4 oz.) chopped nuts
Set aside.

Cream together
   ½ cup butter or margarine, softened
   1 cup sifted confectioners' sugar
   2 teaspoons vanilla extract

Beat until thick and lemon colored and blend
into creamed mixture
   3 egg yolks
Stir in melted chocolate.

Beat until rounded peaks are formed and fold
(page 5) into chocolate mixture
   3 egg whites
Spread one-third crumb mixture in the pan.
Cover with one-half the chocolate mixture,
pressing firmly into crumbs. Repeat, ending with
crumb layer. Chill in refrigerator overnight.

8 servings

—Rum Toffee Dessert

Follow △ Recipe. Substitute 2 teaspoons **rum
extract** for vanilla extract.

Chocolate Mousse

Set refrigerator control at colder operating
temperature. Set a rotary beater and a bowl
in refrigerator to chill.

Pour into a small cup or custard cup
   2 tablespoons cold water
Sprinkle evenly over water
   1½ teaspoons unflavored gelatin
Let stand until softened.

Heat until milk is scalded (page 6) and
chocolate melted
   1 cup milk
   2 oz. (2 sq.) chocolate
Remove from heat. Blend in softened gelatin
stirring until gelatin is completely dissolved.
Stir in
   ¾ cup sugar
   ½ teaspoon salt
Blend well until sugar and salt are dissolved.
Cool. Stir in
   1 teaspoon vanilla extract

Using chilled bowl and beater, whip one cup
at a time until of medium consistency (piles
softly)
   2 cups chilled whipping cream
Fold (page 5) into gelatin mixture. Turn into
refrigerator tray. Place in freezing compartment. Freeze until firm (3 to 4 hrs.). Turn
refrigerator back to normal operating temperature and allow mousse to ripen until ready
to serve.

5 servings

Brown-Edge Wafer Roll

▲ *Base Recipe*

Prepare
   **Creamy Chocolate Frosting
       (page 19)**
Spread a thin layer of filling on each of
   27 brown-edge wafers
Turn wafers on end and press together to
form one long roll made up of alternate layers
of wafers and filling. Cover outside of roll
with remaining filling.

Chill in refrigerator 2 to 3 hrs. Cut into
diagonal slices about 1 in. thick.

6 to 8 servings

—Chocolate Wafer Roll

Follow △ Recipe. Substitute for the Creamy
Chocolate Frosting, 1 cup sweetened **whipped
cream** (page 6). Substitute **Crispy Rolled
Wafers** (page 24) or commercial **chocolate
wafers** for the brown-edge wafers.

—Party Loaf

Double △ Recipe or Chocolate Wafer Roll
recipe. Prepare 9 rolls of alternate wafers and
filling, each made of 6 wafers. Place rolls on
end close together on serving dish to form
loaf 3 rolls long and 3 rolls wide. Cover entire
loaf with remaining filling. Top with moist,
shredded **coconut.** Slice straight across loaf.

About 12 servings

Magic Coconut Nests

Butter six 2½-in. muffin pan wells.

Cook in top of double boiler, stirring frequently, over rapidly boiling water
⅔ cup sweetened condensed milk
1 oz. (1 sq.) chocolate
When mixture is thick (about 10 min.), turn into large bowl. Add and blend well
1 teaspoon vanilla extract
2 cups moist shredded coconut
Place about ¼ cup of mixture in each muffin well. Pack firmly around bottom and sides. Let mixture extend ½ in. above rim of pans.

Bake at 350°F until top edges are browned and firm (about 20 min.). Loosen edges and lift carefully from pans. Cool on rack. Just before serving, fill nests with **vanilla ice cream**. Top with **Peppermint Fudge Sauce Superb** (page 41).   *6 nests*

Chocolate Éclairs or Cream Puffs

Grease a baking sheet.

Combine and bring to boiling
1 cup water
½ cup butter or margarine
¼ teaspoon salt
Add, all at one time, and stir in vigorously
1 cup sifted all-purpose flour
Continue cooking, stirring constantly, until mixture forms a smooth ball which leaves sides of pan clean. Do not overcook. Remove from heat. Add, one at a time, beating until smooth after each addition
4 eggs
Continue beating until mixture is thick and smooth and breaks off when spoon is raised. Drop from spoon onto baking sheet 2 in. apart to allow for spreading. Shape cream puffs in balls with 2 tablespoons or squeeze equivalent amount from pastry bag. Shape éclairs with tablespoons or pastry bag into 4½x1-in. strips.

Bake at 450°F 15 min. Reduce temperature to 350°F and bake 20 to 25 min. longer, or until golden in color. Remove to cooling rack and cool. Cut off top of each shell and fill with green or pink peppermint or vanilla ice cream; replace top and serve with chocolate sauce. Or cut off top and fill with **Cocoa Whipped Cream Filling** (page 19), sweetened **whipped cream** (page 6), **Chocolate Cream Filling** (page 20) or a **custard cream filling**. Replace top. Cover with **chocolate glaze**.
                    1 doz. éclairs or Cream Puffs

Note: Dough may be prepared ahead of time, wrapped in waxed paper, and stored in refrigerator several hours or overnight.

For Chocolate Glaze (*Cooked*)—Melt (page 5) 1 oz. (1 sq.) **chocolate**. Mix in heavy saucepan

¾ cup sifted **confectioners' sugar**, 1 teaspoon **dark corn syrup**, 1 tablespoon **cream**, the melted chocolate, 2 teaspoons **boiling water** and 1 teaspoon **butter**.

Place over low heat and stir constantly until butter melts. Remove from heat and add ½ teaspoon **vanilla extract**. Cool slightly. Spread over tops of eclairs.

For Chocolate Glaze (*Uncooked*) — Blend 1½ cups **confectioners' sugar** into 1 **egg white**. Add ¾ teaspoon **vanilla extract** and 1½ oz. (1½ sq.) **chocolate**, melted (page 5). Mix thoroughly and spread over tops of éclairs.

Steamed Chocolate Pudding

▲ *Base Recipe*

Grease a 1½-qt. mold.

Melt (page 5) and set aside to cool
3 oz. (3 sq.) chocolate

Sift together and set aside
1½ cups sifted all-purpose flour
1½ teaspoons baking powder
½ teaspoon salt

Cream together until shortening is softened
⅔ cup butter
2 teaspoons vanilla extract
Add gradually, creaming until fluffy after each addition
¾ cup plus 2 tablespoons sugar
Add in thirds, beating well after each addition
2 eggs, well beaten
Stir in chocolate. Blend well.

Measure
¾ cup milk
Alternately add dry ingredients in fourths, milk in thirds, to creamed mixture. After each addition, beat only until blended. Finally beat only until batter is smooth (do not overbeat). Turn batter into mold. Cover mold tightly with greased lid or tie on aluminum foil, parchment paper or 2 layers of waxed paper.

Place on trivet or rack in steamer or deep kettle with tight-fitting cover. Pour boiling water into bottom of steamer (enough to continue boiling throughout entire steaming period if possible. Quickly add more boiling water if necessary during cooking period.) Mold should be above the water level. Tightly cover steamer and steam the pudding 1½ hrs., keeping the water boiling at all times.

Remove pudding from steamer. Immediately loosen edges of pudding with spatula. Unmold onto serving plate. If desired, garnish with raisins, pecan halves and candied cherries.

Serve hot, with sweetened, whipped cream (page 6) or Marshmallow Sauce (page 41).
                    6 to 8 servings

—Chocolate-Nut Pudding

Follow △ Recipe. Add and blend in ½ cup (about 2 oz.) coarsely chopped **nuts** before turning batter into mold.

—Rainbow Pudding

Follow △ Recipe. Omit chocolate. Divide batter into 3 parts and put into separate bowls. To one part add 2 or 3 drops **red food coloring** and ½ teaspoon **almond extract**; to the second add 1 oz. (1 sq.) melted and cooled **chocolate**; to the third add a drop or two of either **yellow or green food coloring**, or no coloring. Stir each mixture until blended.

Pour batter into mold in 3 layers. For swirled effect, gently draw a spoon through the layers about 3 times after layers are in mold.

Brownie Waffles

▲ *Base Recipe*

Heat waffle baker while preparing batter.

Put into top of double boiler
> **1½ pkgs. (9 oz.) semi-sweet chocolate pieces**
> **¾ cup milk**
> **½ cup shortening**

Heat over simmering water until chocolate and shortening are melted. Remove from heat and blend thoroughly. Set aside to cool.

Meanwhile, chop and set aside
> **½ cup (2 oz.) nuts**

Sift together into a large bowl and set aside
> **1½ cups sifted cake flour**
> **½ teaspoon baking powder**
> **½ teaspoon salt**

Beat until thick and lemon-colored
> **2 egg yolks**

Add gradually, continuing to beat
> **⅓ cup plus 1 tablespoon sugar**

Beat in chocolate mixture. Add all at one time to sifted dry ingredients; beat until batter is smooth. Blend in the chopped nuts.

Beat until rounded peaks are formed
> **2 egg whites**

Fold (page 5) beaten egg whites into batter.

Unless temperature is automatically shown on waffle baker, test heat with a few drops of cold water; it is hot enough for baking when the water spreads out and bubbles. (If temperature is automatically shown, set control at lowest setting.)

Spoon batter into center of baker, allowing 1 to 2 tablespoons for each section. Lower cover and allow waffle to bake 7 to 8 min., or until steaming stops. Do not raise cover during baking period. Lift cover, loosen waffle with fork and carefully remove one section at a time. Sprinkle with
> **Confectioners' sugar**

Serve hot or cooled.

About 6 servings

—Cherry Brownie Waffles

Follow △ Recipe. Blend in with nuts ½ cup (8-oz. jar) **maraschino cherries**, drained and quartered.

—Brownie Waffle Sundae

Follow △ Recipe. Serve sections of Brownie Waffles topped with **vanilla ice cream** and any **chocolate sauce**.

—Brownie Waffle Sandwiches

Follow △ Recipe. Spread one-half of waffles with **raspberry jam**. Cover with remaining half. Top with sweetened **whipped cream** (page 6).

Budget-Wise Chocolate Ice Cream

Set refrigerator control at colder operating temperature. Set a large bowl and rotary beater in refrigerator to chill.

Pour into a small cup or custard cup
> **2 tablespoons cold water**

Sprinkle evenly over water
> **2 teaspoons unflavored gelatin**

Let stand until softened.

Heat in a heavy saucepan until chocolate is melted
> **1½ oz. (1½ sq.) chocolate**
> **¾ cup water**

Remove hot melted chocolate from range and add softened gelatin. Stir until gelatin is completely dissolved. Cool.

Beat until thick and lemon colored
> **2 egg yolks**
> **6 tablespoons sugar**
> **¼ cup light corn sirup**

Blend in cooled gelatin mixture and
> **1½ cups undiluted evaporated milk**
> **2 teaspoons vanilla extract**

Pour into refrigerator tray and chill in freezing compartment.

When fairly firm, beat with rotary beater until frothy
> **2 egg whites**

Add gradually, beating well after each addition
> **2 tablespoons sugar**

Continue beating until very stiff peaks are formed.

Turn mixture into chilled bowl and beat with chilled rotary beater until fluffy. Fold (page 5) in egg whites and return mixture to refrigerator tray; freeze until firm (2½ to 3 hrs.).

5 or 6 servings

Freezer Chocolate Ice Cream

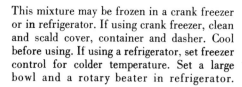

This mixture may be frozen in a crank freezer or in refrigerator. If using crank freezer, clean and scald cover, container and dasher. Cool before using. If using a refrigerator, set freezer control for colder temperature. Set a large bowl and a rotary beater in refrigerator.

Heat in top of double boiler until milk is scalded (page 6) and chocolate melted
1½ cups milk
3 oz. (3 sq.) chocolate
Set aside.

Mix thoroughly
1 cup sugar
¼ cup sifted all-purpose flour
¼ teaspoon salt
Add and blend well
½ cup cold milk
Stir flour mixture into hot milk. While stirring gently and constantly, bring rapidly to boiling over direct heat. Cook until mixture is thickened. Place over simmering water and cover; cook 12 min., stirring occasionally. Vigorously stir about 3 tablespoons of hot mixture into
2 eggs, slightly beaten
Immediately return to cooked mixture. Stirring constantly and rapidly, cook 3 to 5 min. Remove from heat. Cool.

Stir in
4 cups heavy cream
3 tablespoons vanilla extract

For Dasher-Type Freezer—Fill chilled container two-thirds full with ice cream mixture. Cover tightly. Set into freezer tub. (For electric freezer, follow manufacturer's directions.) Fill tub with alternate layers of
8 parts crushed ice
1 part rock salt
Turn handle slowly 5 min. Turn rapidly until handle becomes difficult to turn (about 15 min.). Wipe lid well and remove dasher. Pack down ice cream and cover with waxed paper. Again put lid on top and fill opening for dasher with cork. Repack freezer in ice using
4 parts crushed ice
1 part rock salt
Cover with heavy paper or cloth. Let ripen 2 to 3 hrs.

For Refrigerator—Pour ice cream mixture into refrigerator trays. When mixture becomes mushy, turn into chilled bowl and beat with chilled beater. Beating helps to form fine crystals and give a smooth, creamy mixture. Return to refrigerator until firm.

2 qts. ice cream

Ice Cream Balls

▲ *Base Recipe*

Set refrigerator control at colder operating temperature.

Pack into deep refrigerator tray and freeze until hard
1 qt. ice cream

Crumb enough **Crispy Rolled Wafers** (page 24) to make
1 cup chocolate cookie crumbs
Form ice cream balls with a scoop rinsed each time in hot water. Roll each ball in crumbs until thickly coated.

Place balls in shallow refrigerator tray and freeze until serving time.

6 to 8 servings

—Floating Snowballs

Follow △ Recipe. Omit cookie crumbs and substitute 1 cup moist, shredded **coconut**. Roll balls in coconut: chill. Spoon **Marshmallow Sauce** (page 41) into serving dishes and float a coconut ball in the sauce.

Chocolate Parfait

▲ *Base Recipe*

Set refrigerator control at colder operating temperature. Set a rotary beater and a bowl in refrigerator to chill.

Melt (page 5) and set aside to cool
2 oz. (2 sq.) chocolate

Mix in saucepan
1 cup sugar
1 cup water
Cook to 238°F (soft ball stage, page 6; remove from heat while testing).

Shortly before sirup is cooked, beat until stiff, not dry, peaks are formed
3 egg whites
Pour sirup in fine stream over egg whites, beating constantly until mixture is cool.
Using chilled bowl and beater, whip one cup at a time until of medium consistency (piles softly)
2 cups chilled whipping cream
Blend melted chocolate and whipped cream into cooled egg white mixture with
1½ tablespoons vanilla extract
Pour into refrigerator trays or molds and place in freezing compartment and freeze 3 to 4 hrs.; or pour into mold to overflowing, cover with waxed paper, and press cover down tightly over paper. Pack in a mixture of one part ice and four parts rock salt. Freeze 3 to 4 hrs.

1¼ qts. parfait

—Peppermint Parfait

Follow △ Recipe. Add 1 cup crushed **peppermint-stick candy** or ½ teaspoon **peppermint extract** when folding ingredients into cooled egg white mixture.

Frozen Cocoa Marlow

▲ Base Recipe

Set refrigerator control at colder operating temperature. Set a rotary beater and a bowl in refrigerator to chill.

Cut into quarters (page 5) and set aside
  32 (½ lb.) marshmallows

Slowly blend together
  ½ cup cocoa
  2 cups milk
Combine with marshmallows and heat over simmering water, stirring occasionally until well blended. Stir in
  1½ teaspoons vanilla extract
  Few grains salt
Cool until slightly stiffened. Using chilled bowl and beater, whip until of medium consistency (piles softly) and combine with marshmallow mixture
  1 cup chilled whipping cream
Pour into refrigerator tray. Freeze about 4 hrs.
6 to 8 servings

—Frozen Choco-Mint Marlow

Follow △ Recipe or Frozen Chocolate Marlow, below. Add ¼ teaspoon **peppermint extract**, or ¼ cup crushed **peppermint-stick candy** with the whipped cream.

—Frozen Chocolate Marlow

Follow △ Recipe. For cocoa, substitute 2 oz. (2 sq.) **chocolate**, melted (page 5). Stir in marshmallows and milk.

Chiffon Refrigerator Cake

Place a rotary beater and a bowl in refrigerator to chill.

Pour into a refrigerator tray
  1⅓ cups undiluted evaporated milk
Set in freezing compartment until ice crystals form around edges.

Line bottom and sides of 9-in. spring-form pan with
  Ladyfingers (about 36)
Set aside.

Mix thoroughly in the top of a double boiler
  1 env. unflavored gelatin
  ½ cup sugar
Beat together in a bowl until well blended
  6 egg yolks
  1¼ cups cream
  ¼ teaspoon salt
Combine with the gelatin mixture in top of double boiler. Set over boiling water and cook, stirring occasionally, about 5 min., or until gelatin is completely dissolved. Remove from heat and stir in until the chocolate is melted
  1 pkg. (12 oz.) semi-sweet chocolate pieces
  4 teaspoons rum extract
  2 teaspoons vanilla extract

Chill in refrigerator or in a pan of ice and water until mixture mounds slightly when dropped from a spoon. (If mixture is placed over ice and water, stir frequently; if placed in refrigerator, stir occasionally.)

When the mixture begins to thicken, beat until frothy
  6 egg whites
Add about 2 tablespoons at a time, beating well after each addition
  ½ cup sugar
Beat until very stiff peaks are formed.

Spread thickened gelatin mixture over beaten egg whites and fold (page 5) gently until thoroughly blended.
Turn the chilled evaporated milk into the chilled bowl and beat with electric beater on medium speed until stiff peaks are formed.

Add and continue beating until thoroughly blended
  2 tablespoons lemon juice
Whip until stiff.

Gently fold (page 5) into gelatin mixture. Turn into prepared pan. Chill about 8 hrs., or until set.
10 to 12 servings

Chocolate Refrigerator Cake

Place a small bowl and a rotary beater in refrigerator to chill.

Line bottom and sides of 9-in. spring-form pan with
  Ladyfingers or vanilla or chocolate wafers (about 3 doz. for entire cake)

Melt (page 5)
  6 oz. sweet chocolate
in
  ⅓ cup water
Stir and set aside to cool

Chop and set aside
  ½ cup (2 oz.) nuts

Beat with rotary beater until thick and lemon colored
  4 egg yolks
Blend in thoroughly the cooled chocolate and
  3 tablespoons sugar
  1 teaspoon vanilla extract
Chill mixture in refrigerator.

Using chilled bowl and beater, beat until of medium consistency (piles softly)
  1 cup chilled whipping cream

Beat until rounded peaks are formed
  4 egg whites
Gently fold (page 5) whipped cream and egg whites into chocolate mixture. Pour one-half into prepared pan. Cover with remaining ladyfingers or wafers. Pour remainder of chocolate mixture over top.

Refrigerate about 8 hrs., or until set. If desired, garnish top with **whipped cream** and chopped **nuts**.
10 to 12 servings

Toppers and Sauces

Chocolate Toppers

▲ *Base Mix Recipe*

Toppers to add the mouth-watering touch.

Mix together
- 2 tablespoons sugar
- 2 tablespoons cocoa or grated chocolate
- 1 teaspoon cinnamon

—Doughnut Topper

Roll warm doughnuts in △ Mix.

—Cookie Topper

Sprinkle △ Mix over sugar cookies before baking.

—Coffee Cake Topper

Prepare △ Mix, increasing sugar and cocoa to 4 tablespoons each. Blend in 2 tablespoons **flour** and cut in with pastry blender 2 tablespoons **butter** or **margarine**. Sprinkle on top of unbaked coffee cake.

—Toast Topper

Prepare △ Mix and cream with it 1 tablespoon softened **butter** or **margarine**. Toast one side of **bread slices**; spread mix on untoasted sides. Broil 4 in. from heat source until bubbly.

Bittersweet Chocolate Sauce

▲ *Base Recipe*

Heat together in the top of a double boiler over hot (not simmering) water, stirring frequently until sauce is smooth
- 1 pkg. (12 oz.) semi-sweet chocolate
- 2 oz. (2 sq.) chocolate
- 1 cup whipping cream
- 1 teaspoon vanilla extract

Serve hot over ice cream for sundaes. The sauce may be stored, covered, in the refrigerator and reheated. *2 cups sauce*

—Semi-Sweet Chocolate Sauce

Follow △ Recipe; omit unsweetened chocolate. Heat the cream and ¾ cup **sugar** together in a heavy saucepan, stirring frequently until sugar is completely dissolved. Meanwhile, start melting semi-sweet chocolate (page 5). When chocolate is partially melted, remove from heat and add hot cream mixture and vanilla extract; stir until smooth.

Blender Chocolate-Rum Sauce

Put into electric blender container in order listed
- ⅓ cup warm water
- ½ cup sugar
- 4 teaspoons nonfat dry milk solids
- 2 oz. (2 sq.) chocolate, cut in small pieces
- 1 tablespoon butter or margarine
- ¼ teaspoon rum extract
- ⅛ teaspoon salt

Cover, turn on motor and blend ingredients about 1 min. Turn off motor. Scrape down sides of container with rubber spatula so ingredients will become evenly mixed. Cover and blend about 3 min. more, or until sauce is smooth, creamy and thick. Store in covered jar in refrigerator.

¾ cup sauce

Cocoa Sirup

▲ *Base Recipe*

Mix thoroughly
- 2 cups sugar
- 1 cup cocoa

Stir in to make a paste
- ½ cup water

Stir into
- 2 cups boiling water

Let boil for 6 min. Remove from heat.

Stir in
- ¼ teaspoon salt

Cool sirup. Store in tightly covered jar in refrigerator.

About 2 cups sirup

—Chocolate Sirup

Follow △ Recipe. Substitute for cocoa 6 oz. (6 sq.) **chocolate**, grated. Omit ½ cup water.

—Mocha Cocoa Sirup

Follow △ Recipe. Substitute **double-strength coffee beverage** for ½ cup water.

Congo Hard Sauce

▲ *Base Recipe*

Melt (page 5) and set aside to cool
- ⅓ pkg. (2 oz.) semi-sweet chocolate pieces

Cream until shortening is softened
- ¼ cup butter or margarine
- ½ teaspoon vanilla extract
- ⅛ teaspoon salt

Cream in gradually
- ⅔ cup sifted confectioners' sugar

Blend in chocolate and stir until smooth and well mixed. Add and blend thoroughly

 ⅓ cup sifted confectioners' sugar

More sugar may be added if a stiffer hard sauce is desired.

About ⅔ cup sauce

—Chocolate Hard Sauce

Follow △ Recipe. Substitute 1 oz. (1 sq.) melted **chocolate** for semi-sweet pieces. Add ½ teaspoon **rum** or **brandy extract**.

—Cocoa Hard Sauce

Follow △ Recipe. Omit semi-sweet pieces. Sift ⅓ cup **cocoa** with all of the sifted confectioner's sugar. Increase butter or margarine to ⅓ cup.

Bittersweet Chocolate Sauce

 ▲ *Base Recipe*

Heat in top of double boiler until chocolate is melted (page 5) and milk scalded (page 6)

 4 oz. (4 sq.) chocolate
 ¾ cup milk

Stir well. Blend in thoroughly

 1 cup sugar
 ¼ teaspoon salt

Remove double boiler top and place over direct heat. Cook about 2 min., stirring constantly, to dissolve sugar and thicken sauce. Remove from heat and blend in

 ¼ cup butter or margarine
 ½ teaspoon almond extract

Serve hot or cold.

About 2 cups sauce

—Choco-Almond Topping

Follow △ Recipe. Stir in with the butter ½ cup (about 2½ oz.) blanched and toasted (page 5) **almonds**, slivered.

—Choco-Raisin Topping

Follow △ Recipe. Stir in ½ cup (about 2 oz.) **raisins** with the butter.

—Chocolate Whipped Cream Sauce

Follow △ Recipe and thoroughly chill sauce. Fold 1 cup **whipping cream**, whipped, into sauce before serving.

About 4 cups sauce

Marshmallow Sauce

Melt (page 5)

 3 oz. (3 sq.) chocolate

Stir in

 ⅓ cup cream

When well blended, add

 16 (¼ lb.) marshmallows

Continue heating, stirring occasionally, until marshmallows are melted and sauce is thoroughly blended. Serve cold.

1½ cups sauce

Fudge Sauce Superb

 ▲ *Base Recipe*

Combine in saucepan

 2 cups firmly packed brown sugar
 1 cup cream
 3 oz. (3 sq.) chocolate
 3 tablespoons butter or margarine

Cook gently, stirring occasionally, to 234°F (soft ball stage, page 6; remove from heat while testing). Add

 1 teaspoon vanilla extract

Beat 1 min. Serve hot or cold.

About 1½ cups sauce

—Cocoa Fudge Sauce Superb

Follow △ Recipe. Substitute ¾ cup **cocoa** for the chocolate; mix with brown sugar before adding butter and cream.

—Peppermint Fudge Sauce Superb

Follow △ Recipe. Stir in 2 or 3 drops **peppermint extract** with the vanilla extract.

—Peanut Fudge Sauce Superb

Follow △ Recipe. Stir in ¼ cup **peanut butter** or ¼ cup (1 oz.) finely chopped **peanuts** after removing from heat.

Orange Chocolate Sauce

Melt (page 5)

 1 oz. (1 sq.) chocolate

Meanwhile, mix thoroughly in top of a double boiler

 ½ cup sugar
 ⅓ cup nonfat dry milk solids
 1 tablespoon cornstarch
 ⅛ teaspoon salt

Add gradually, stirring until smooth

 1 cup water

Blend in melted chocolate. Stirring gently and constantly, bring rapidly to boiling over direct heat. Reduce heat; cook and stir for 3 min. Place over simmering water. Cover and cook about 12 min., stirring 3 or 4 times. Remove from simmering water. Blend in

 2 tablespoons orange juice
 1 tablespoon butter or margarine
 1 teaspoon grated orange peel
 (page 5)

Cool and chill in refrigerator. Serve cold.

About 1½ cups sauce

Beverages

Chocolate Eggnog

▲ *Base Recipe*

Nutritious eggnog blended with chocolate spells sheer delight to hungry children and adults, too.

Beat until thick and lemon colored
> **6 egg yolks**

Add, blending well
> **6 cups chilled, rich milk, or one-half milk and one-half cream**
> **1½ cups Chocolate or Cocoa Sirup (page 40)**
> **1 tablespoon vanilla extract**

Beat until rounded peaks are formed
> **6 egg whites**

Fold (page 5) beaten egg whites into milk mixture. Serve cold in mugs or in tall glasses. If desired, sprinkle with
> **Dash of nutmeg**

8 servings

—Banananog

Peel and slice 6 brown-flecked **bananas** into bowl and beat with hand rotary beater or electric mixer until creamy. Fold in beaten egg white and proceed as in △ Recipe.

Chocolate Soda, Home-Style

Blend together in a tall glass
> **1 small scoop softened ice cream**
> **2 to 4 tablespoons Chocolate or Cocoa Sirup (page 40)**

Pour over ice cream
> **½ cup cold milk**
> **½ cup sparkling water or ginger ale**

Beat but do not shake to blend well.

Float in soda mixture
> **1 or 2 scoops softened ice cream**

Serve immediately.

1 large serving

Minty Chocolate Flip

Combine and stir until smooth
> **¼ cup malted milk powder**
> **¼ cup Chocolate or Cocoa Sirup (page 40)**

Blend in slowly
> **2 cups cold milk**
> **1½ teaspoons vanilla extract**
> **½ teaspoon peppermint extract**
> **¼ teaspoon salt**

Beat or shake well. Chill in refrigerator. When ready to serve, pour into shaker and add
> **2 cups (1 pt.) vanilla ice cream**

Shake until smooth. Top with **whipped cream.**

6 servings

Hot Chocolate

▲ *Base Recipe*

Mix together and cook over low heat, stirring constantly
> **2 oz. (2 sq.) chocolate**
> **¾ cup water**
> **5 to 6 tablespoons sugar**
> **⅛ teaspoon salt**

When chocolate is melted, increase heat and boil 3 min., stirring constantly. Reduce heat.

Gradually stir in
> **3¼ cups milk**

Heat to scalding. Do not boil. Stir in
> **1 teaspoon vanilla extract**

6 servings

—Hot Cocoa

Follow △ Recipe. Substitute 6 tablespoons **cocoa** for chocolate. Blend cocoa and sugar before adding water.

—Mocha Chocolate

Follow △ Recipe. Substitute ¾ cup **double-strength coffee beverage** for ¾ cup of the milk. Add ¼ teaspoon **cinnamon**, if desired.

—Mint Chocolate

Follow △ Recipe. Substitute 8 **chocolate-covered peppermint patties** for the chocolate and sugar.

—Honey Hot Chocolate or Cocoa

Follow △ Recipe or Hot Cocoa recipe. Substitute an equal amount of **honey** for the sugar in either recipe.

—Quick Hot Chocolate or Cocoa

Stir 1½ to 2 tablespoons of **Chocolate Sirup** or **Cocoa Sirup** (page 40) into each cup of scalded milk.

—Chocolate or Cocoa Cooler

Stir 1½ to 2 tablespoons of **Chocolate Sirup** or **Cocoa Sirup** (page 40) into each glass of cold milk. Add cracked **ice**, if desired.

Candies

Chocolate Fudge

▲ *Base Recipe*

Butter a 9-in. square pan.

Combine in a heavy 3-qt. saucepan
- **1⅓ cups milk**
- **4 oz. (4 sq.) chocolate**

Stir over low heat until chocolate is melted. Do not allow mixture to boil. Stir in
- **4 cups sugar**
- **2 tablespoons light corn sirup**
- **½ teaspoon salt**

Cook slowly, stirring until sugar is dissolved. Increase heat to medium and bring mixture to boiling.

Cook, stirring occasionally, to 234°F (soft ball stage, page 6; remove from heat while testing). Using a pastry brush dipped in water, wash down the crystals from sides of saucepan from time to time during cooking. Remove mixture from heat and cool to lukewarm (about 110°F) without stirring or jarring the saucepan. Then add
- **¼ cup butter or margarine**
- **4 teaspoons vanilla extract**

Beat vigorously until mixture is dull in color. Quickly turn into the buttered pan without scraping bottom and sides of saucepan and spread evenly. Set aside to cool. When firm, cut into 1½-in. squares.

36 pieces fudge

—Peanut Butter Fudge

Follow △ Recipe. Substitute 8 tablespoons **peanut butter** for butter.

—Cocoa Fudge

Follow △ Recipe. Substitute ¾ cup **cocoa** for chocolate. Blend cocoa with sugar before adding milk.

—Pecan Fudge

Follow △ Recipe. Before pouring, add 2 cups (about 8 oz.) chopped **pecans.**

—Tutti-Frutti Fudge

Follow △ Recipe. Before pouring, add ⅓ cup each: **candied cherries, candied pineapple, raisins.**

—Marshmallow Fudge

Follow △ Recipe. Before pouring, add 32 (½ lb.) quartered **marshmallows (page 5)** with butter.

Hasty Chocolate Caramels

Set out candy thermometer. Butter an 8-in. square pan.

Heat in heavy saucepan over lowest heat
- **3 oz. (3 sq.) chocolate**
- **1¼ cups (14-oz. can) sweetened condensed milk**
- **½ cup light or dark corn sirup**
- **⅛ teaspoon salt**

Set candy thermometer (page 6) in place. Stirring constantly, cook mixture (about 20 min.) to 235°F (this particular mixture tends to form a firm ball rather than the usual soft ball at 235°F, page 6; remove from heat while testing). The consistency of the ball will be the consistency of the finished product. Cook longer if desired. The higher the temperature reached, the firmer the candy. Candy cooked beyond 244°F will be too brittle. Stir in one tablespoon at a time
- **3 tablespoons butter or margarine**

Mix in
- **½ cup (about 2 oz.) chopped nuts such as almonds, blanched (page 5)**
- **2 teaspoons vanilla extract**

Turn into buttered pan without scraping bottom or sides of saucepan. Cool until lukewarm.

Loosen sides and turn candy onto cutting board. Cut into 6 strips. Work each strip with hands into roll. Cut each roll into 1-in. pieces. Wrap in waxed or glassine paper and store in a tightly covered container.

About 4 doz. caramels

Coconut Kisses

Line baking sheet with waxed paper.

Blend together in a bowl
- **½ cup (1 or 2) hot riced or mashed potatoes (somewhat packed in cup)**
- **1 tablespoon butter**

Beat in thoroughly
- **3½ cups (1 lb.) confectioners' sugar, sifted**
- **⅛ teaspoon salt**
- **2 teaspoons vanilla extract**

Mix in
- **3 tablespoons cocoa, sifted, or 1 oz. (1 sq.) chocolate, melted (page 5)**

Then blend in
- **3 cups (1 lb.) moist, shredded coconut**

Drop by teaspoonfuls onto paper-lined sheet. Set kisses in a cool place to harden. Store in tightly covered container.

About 1½ lbs, kisses

Quick Four-Way Fudge

▲ Base Recipe

Butter an 8x8x2-in. pan, line with waxed paper cut to fit bottom; butter again.

Melt (page 5)
> **1 pkg. (12 oz.) semi-sweet chocolate pieces**

Blend in
> **1¼ cups (14-oz. can) sweetened condensed milk**

Remove from heat and stir in
> **2 teaspoons vanilla extract**

Pour into pan and sprinkle top with
> **½ to 1 cup (2 to 4 oz.) chopped nuts**

Chill in refrigerator about 4 hrs. or until firm.

When firm, cut into 64 1-in. squares.

About 1¼ lbs. fudge

—Fudge Patties

Follow △ Recipe, omitting chopped nuts. Shape cooled (not chilled) squares into small balls. Flatten; press a whole **nutmeat** in center of each.

—Fudge Miniatures

Follow △ Recipe; set out a cookie sheet in place of an 8x8-in. pan and line with waxed paper. With vanilla add 3 cups of any one or any mixture of these: crisp **rice cereal, corn flakes, seedless raisins,** unsalted chopped **nuts** or moist shredded **coconut.** Drop by teaspoonfuls onto waxed paper and put in cool place to set.

—Fudge Balls

Follow △ Recipe. With vanilla extract add 2 cups of any one or any mixture of these: **seedless raisins,** unsalted chopped **nuts** or moist, shredded **coconut.** Turn into pan and cool. When firm enough to handle, cut into squares. Shape into small balls and roll in finely chopped **coconut** or **nuts.**

Chocolate Divinity

Creamy texture and smooth flavor justify the time spent in making this divinity.

Lightly butter baking sheet. Set out candy thermometer.

Melt (page 5) and set aside to cool
> **2 oz. (2 sq.) chocolate**

Combine in saucepan over medium heat, stirring only until mixture begins to boil
> **2 cups sugar**
> **⅔ cup water**
> **½ cup light corn sirup**
> **¼ teaspoon salt**

Cover and cook 5 min. (This helps to dissolve any crystals that may have formed on sides of pan.) Remove cover and set candy thermometer (page 6) in place. Boil mixture without stirring. During cooking, wash any crystals from sides of saucepan with a pastry brush dipped in water.

Shortly before sirup reaches 252°F (hard ball stage, page 6; remove from heat while testing), using high speed on electric mixer, beat in large bowl until stiff, not dry, peaks are formed
> **3 egg whites**

When the sirup reaches 252°F, immediately pour sirup in a fine stream onto stiffly beaten egg whites, beating constantly using high speed. In the early stage, the mass flows down from beater in a continuous ribbon. Continue beating until mixture no longer flows but holds its shape (about 35 min.). At this point, quickly blend in cooled chocolate and
> **1 teaspoon vanilla extract**

Drop by teaspoonfuls onto baking sheet.

Store in tightly covered container.

About 48 pieces divinity

Toffee

Kitchen magic—when nuts are chopped in an electric blender for this butter-rich candy.

Set out candy thermometer. Butter a 15½x 10½x1-in. jelly-roll pan.

Blanch, toast and salt (page 5)
> **11 oz. (about 2 cups) almonds**

Coarsely chop the almonds and set aside.

Start melting in a heavy 2-qt. saucepan over low heat
> **2 cups butter**

Add gradually, stirring constantly
> **2 cups sugar**

Blend in 1 cup almonds and
> **6 tablespoons water**
> **2 tablespoons light corn sirup**

Set candy thermometer in place. Cook over medium heat, stirring a few times, until temperature reaches 300°F.

Remove from heat, remove thermometer and stir in
> **1 teaspoon vanilla extract**

Quickly pour into the prepared pan and spread to corners.

When candy has cooled slightly, mark into squares with a sharp knife. Cool.

Meanwhile, melt (page 5) and cool
> **8 oz. milk chocolate or semi-sweet chocolate**

When candy is completely cool, spread melted chocolate evenly over top. Sprinkle remaining almonds over chocolate.

When chocolate is set, break toffee into pieces. Store in tightly covered container between layers of waxed paper, aluminum foil or moisture-vaporproof material.

About 3 lbs. Toffee

Creamy Cocoa Taffy

Butter a large shallow pan or platter. Set out candy thermometer.

Mix thoroughly in heavy saucepan
**2¼ cups sugar
1½ cups light corn sirup
⅔ cup Dutch process cocoa
4 teaspoons cider vinegar
¼ teaspoon salt**
Cook slowly, stirring constantly, until sugar dissolves. Bring mixture to a boil; add slowly so boiling does not stop
½ cup undiluted evaporated milk

Hang candy thermometer on pan so bulb does not touch side or bottom of pan.

Cook mixture over medium heat, stirring constantly, until temperature of mixture is 248°F (firm ball stage, page 6; remove from heat while testing).

Immediately pour mixture into buttered pan.

When cool enough to handle, pull in cool place, a small portion at a time, (with buttered hands) until candy is lighter in color and no longer sticky to the touch. Twist pulled strip slightly and place on waxed paper or board. Cut with scissors into 1-in. pieces. Wrap in waxed or glassine paper. Store in a tightly covered container in a cool, dry place.

About 2 lbs. taffy

Pecan Crunch

Butter a 10-in. square pan. Set out a candy thermometer.

Finely chop and reserve ½ cup
1 cup (about 4 oz.) pecans
Mix the remaining nuts with
**1 cup (about 4 oz.) coarsely broken
    pecans
1 teaspoon baking soda**
Set mixture aside.

Prepare a sirup by combining in a heavy 2-qt. saucepan
**2¼ cups sugar
1½ cups butter or margarine
½ cup water
1 tablespoon cider vinegar
1 teaspoon salt**
Cook slowly, stirring constantly, until sugar is dissolved.

Set candy thermometer (page 6) in place.

Boil, without stirring, to 290°F (soft crack stage, page 6, if a candy thermometer is not available; remove from heat while testing).

Add pecan-soda mixture to sirup, stirring just enough to blend. Pour into buttered pan and cool on cooling rack.

When cooled, melt (page 5)
4 oz. milk chocolate
Spread the melted chocolate over candy and sprinkle with the reserved pecans.

Turn candy out of pan when chocolate is set. Cut into pieces. Store in tightly covered container between waxed paper layers.

About 2 lbs. crunch

Index